1

Crafting Freedom:
The Infinite-Curiosity Approach

Introduction to Open World Game Design

The Evolution of Open World Games

The journey of open world games has been all about giving players more freedom and bringing richer stories to life. Back in the mid-1980s, games like "The Legend of Zelda" introduced players to big worlds where they could explore at their own pace. This laid the foundation for games that allowed people to wander and interact without following a strict path. However, it was only with the rise of 3D graphics and improved gaming technology that developers could create truly vast and detailed game worlds filled with stories and choices.

As technology improved, open world games became more complex. A game like "Grand Theft Auto III" changed everything by creating a vibrant city where players could interact with all sorts of characters and elements. This was a significant step forward, as it allowed for more lifelike interactions with non-player characters (NPCs). Game designers began to realize that when players engaged with NPCs who responded to their actions, it made the gaming experience feel more meaningful, as if their choices really mattered.

The ways players explore these game worlds have also evolved to enhance storytelling. Developers started using techniques that encourage players to discover stories hidden within the environments. For instance, in "The Elder Scrolls V: Skyrim," players could find rich histories and side quests that seamlessly connected to the main story. This made exploring the world feel rewarding and showed that the game environment itself could tell stories through its design.

Emotional engagement has emerged as a crucial element in the design of open-world games, transforming how narratives are experienced by players. Designers have acknowledged that players' choices must resonate deeply within the game, exerting a significant influence not only on immediate gameplay but also on the overarching storyline.

For instance, "The Witcher 3: Wild Hunt," a benchmark in the genre, illustrates this approach masterfully. The game's vast narrative landscape allows players to navigate a rich tapestry of interconnected story paths, each filled with intricate moral dilemmas and complex character relationships. Players aren't just passive observers; they actively shape the narrative through decisions that can lead to vastly different outcomes.

This dynamic creates a sense of agency that resonates beyond the game's immediate context. The emotional weight of decisions—whether to spare a life or bestow mercy on a character—culminates in a deeper, immersive experience that thoroughly invests players in the fates of the characters and the world itself. As a result, each player's journey is uniquely tailored, replete with personal trials and triumphs that enhance the overall emotional gravitas of the experience.

Looking forward, the future of open world games lies in even better technology and storytelling techniques. As gaming technology keeps advancing, the possibilities for creating more meaningful interactions and storylines will expand. Game designers will continue to explore new ways to enhance emotional connections and make exploration more interesting. The evolution of open world games is an ongoing adventure, inviting creators to push boundaries while emphasizing player freedom and engaging narratives.

Defining Freedom in Game Design

Understanding freedom in video game design, especially in open world games, is about balancing how much players can do on their own with how the story unfolds. Freedom isn't just about giving players a big map to wander; it's about allowing them to make meaningful choices that connect with their feelings and experiences. Game designers need to think about how these choices affect the story and how players enjoy the game. This idea of freedom shapes everything from how the game is played to how characters react to players.

In open world games, freedom shows up in how players explore the world around them. Designers should create settings that encourage curiosity, letting players discover hidden quests, interesting stories, or character interactions that make the game deeper. It's important that the world tells its own story, not just through scripted events, but by the environment itself. When designers embed story elements in the game world, players feel more in control and can connect their exploration to the emotions tied to the narrative.

Interactions with non-playable characters (NPCs) play a crucial role in creating a sense of freedom and agency in video games. Designers are increasingly leveraging advanced technologies, such as artificial intelligence and machine learning, to develop NPCs that behave and respond in ways that feel authentic and integral to the game's storyline. When NPCs are equipped with distinct personalities, backstories, and motivations, players can engage in more meaningful interactions that reflect their choices and actions.

For example, a player might encounter a villager who reacts differently based on the player's previous decisions, such as whether they chose to help others or prioritize their own goals. This variation in response adds layers of depth to the gameplay experience, making players feel more invested in the narrative.

Moreover, this complexity enhances immersion by allowing players to influence the game world actively. It creates a dynamic environment where decisions can lead to long-lasting effects, such as altering alliances, changing story outcomes, or even affecting the game's ending. As a result, players are not merely passive participants; their actions have real consequences, reinforcing the idea that every choice matters in shaping their unique gaming experience.

Emotional engagement is another crucial part of what freedom means in these games. The choices players make should resonate with them personally, influencing their connection to both the narrative and the game world. Designers can create systems that remember player decisions, showing how these choices affect relationships with characters, the state of the game world, and even the ending. This helps players feel invested in their journey, as their freedom to choose impacts their experiences in the game.

Lastly, having multiple story paths is vital for creating a gameplay experience that feels free and open. Designers need to ensure that choices lead to different outcomes, encouraging players to replay the game and explore new storylines. This requires careful planning to understand how various plotlines can connect or change based on what players decide. By focusing on these aspects, game designers can create open-world experiences that celebrate freedom while still maintaining a rich story, leading to more engaging gameplay that resonates with players.

The Importance of Narrative Depth

Narrative depth in open world games is really important for making the gaming experience more exciting and engaging. It's like the heart of the game, providing players with a variety of stories that are woven into the game's setting and actions. In a game where players can roam freely and make their own choices, the story needs to be strong enough to allow different paths and endings. This depth gives players the chance to create their own adventures, forming a personal bond with the world and its characters. When meaningful stories are built into the game, it turns gameplay from just a set of tasks into an emotional journey that players remember even after they've finished playing.

Additionally, well-developed non-playable characters (NPCs) play a key role in enhancing the story. In many games, NPCs are just there to give quests or information, but in a thoughtfully designed open world, these characters can have their own rich backgrounds, motivations, and evolving stories that change based on what players do. This leads to genuine interactions and makes the world feel more real, helping players become more invested in their journey. When NPCs have depth, they can show how player actions affect the world, making the storytelling more immersive.

Exploration in open world games is also crucial for uncovering the story. Instead of just being a way to move around, exploration can reveal deeper narratives, histories, and character developments. By including things like hidden treasures, interesting places, and subtle hints in the environment, game designers can inspire players to investigate further into the story. This not only offers rewards for exploring but also promotes a sense of curiosity and discovery, making players feel like they are actively participating in the story as they learn about the world's background.

Emotional engagement is another important factor for creating narrative depth. When players face choices that affect the story and its characters, they are more likely to connect emotionally with the game. Designers can create situations that evoke feelings of empathy, conflict, and tough choices, prompting players to think about the consequences of their actions. This emotional connection enhances the overall experience and leads to unforgettable moments. By allowing players to make choices that resonate personally, designers can craft stories that stick with them long after the game is over.

Having multiple story paths is essential in crafting engaging open world games that captivate players for hours on end. By providing players with the freedom to make choices that affect the course of their narratives, game designers create a profound sense of agency and control that is crucial in these expansive environments. Each decision, whether minor or monumental, can lead to a variety of outcomes and interactions, allowing for a unique experience that resonates deeply with each player's personal preferences and values.

This diversity in storytelling not only encourages players to replay the game in pursuit of different endings but also cultivates a spirit of exploration and experimentation. As players navigate through various storylines, they encounter new characters, hidden quests, and alternative events that enrich their understanding of the game world and its intricate lore. These diverging paths often unveil hidden motivations of characters and the historical context of the game world, adding layers of complexity to the narrative.

Ultimately, the depth of the narrative transforms open world games into vibrant platforms for dynamic storytelling. This immersive experience makes each player's journey distinctly meaningful, ensuring that every playthrough can yield fresh discoveries and emotional connections, thus enhancing the overall engagement and longevity of the game. By thoughtfully integrating branching narratives, designers unlock a richer gameplay experience that resonates with a diverse audience, catering to both casual players and seasoned gamers alike.

Building a Framework for Narrative-Driven Open Worlds

Core Elements of Storytelling in Open Worlds

Storytelling in open world games is all about creating a lively and immersive environment where players can explore, interact, and make choices that shape their own experiences. Unlike traditional games with a set storyline, open world games offer a flexible framework that invites players to discover the story at their own pace. Designers need to think carefully about how to weave different parts of the story throughout the game world so that every area and interaction adds something meaningful to the overall narrative. This includes integrating background information, developing characters, and using the environment to tell stories, all of which enhance the player's adventure.

Interactions with non-playable characters (NPCs) are crucial for building a rich storytelling experience in these games. Creating smart AI that can engage players in natural conversations can greatly enhance emotional connections. NPCs shouldn't just offer quests; they should also develop relationships and conflicts based on the choices players make. When NPCs respond in thoughtful ways to player decisions, it makes the game world feel alive and responsive, adding depth to the story and increasing the stakes.

Exploration is also key in these open worlds. Players should feel excited to explore and uncover hidden stories, with rewards that help them understand the game's lore and setting better. Designers can use techniques like visual clues, interesting artifacts, and clever world design to guide players towards deeper narratives. Adding dynamic elements like changing weather or landscapes can further enrich the experience, allowing players to engage more personally with the game.

Emotional engagement is vital for successful storytelling. Designers need to think about how choices affect the player's feelings, creating scenarios that spark empathy, conflict, or joy. By offering complex dilemmas and tough decisions, they can draw players into a narrative that feels personal. When players see the consequences of their choices reflected in the game world, it makes their decisions feel important and impactful, giving them a sense of control.

Ultimately, having multiple story paths and outcomes ignites players' interest and passion for the game. When players can choose different directions and witness varied endings, it enriches their journey and armors each experience with uniqueness. This necessitates meticulous planning to weave all the diverse storylines into a cohesive tapestry. Designers aspire for players to truly feel that their choices mold the game world, cultivating a richer and more captivating storytelling adventure in open world games.

Integrating Narrative with Gameplay Mechanics

Creating a captivating open-world video game involves blending storytelling with gameplay in a way that draws players in and makes them feel connected. When a game tells a story alongside its play mechanics, it allows players to shape the narrative through their choices and actions, making each experience unique. Game designers should understand that a story isn't just a background element; it is vital to every part of the player's adventure.

One effective way for designers to tell stories is through environmental storytelling. This means that narrative elements are placed directly within the game world. Players can discover stories by exploring their surroundings—like finding items, noticing how areas are arranged, or interacting with non-player characters (NPCs). This method encourages players to engage with the world around them and fosters a sense of curiosity, as they piece together the story on their own. It enhances immersion and allows players to form a deeper emotional connection with the game.

Dynamic interactions with NPCs also play a crucial role in tying storytelling to gameplay. Designers can create AI characters that respond to players' choices and actions, making the story feel more personal. If NPCs remember how players interacted with them and change their behavior based on that, it builds a more lively and responsive world. This not only makes the game more engaging emotionally but also allows players to experience different story outcomes depending on their decisions, enriching the gameplay experience.

Exploration is another key aspect of storytelling in open-world games. Designers should encourage players to stray off the main path, rewarding their curiosity with narrative-rich content. This could mean discovering hidden quests, lore-filled locations, or special interactions that are only available through exploration. By weaving these elements into the gameplay, designers can make the experience more rewarding. The thrill of uncovering stories while exploring can lead to unforgettable moments that linger in players' minds long after they finish the game.

Ultimately, games have the incredible potential to forge profound emotional connections with players. Designers should embrace the idea that gameplay choices can stir feelings, helping players form bonds with characters and narratives. Choices with significance, moral dilemmas, and visible consequences should mirror the emotional complexity of the story. When gameplay harmonizes with the emotions and stakes of the narrative, it creates unforgettable moments that resonate deeply, making players feel truly invested in the outcomes of their choices. This emotional depth not only elevates gameplay but also enriches the overall story, empowering open-world games to leave a lasting legacy.

Designing Environments that Tell a Story

Creating environments that tell a story is an essential part of making open world games that connect deeply with players. In these vast game worlds, everything from buildings and landscapes to sounds and interactions with characters plays a role in the overall story. Game designers aim to blend storytelling into the environment, allowing players to uncover details about the world and its characters as they explore, rather than just through dialogue or cutscenes. This method encourages players to engage with the world naturally, piecing together narratives through their own discoveries.

One effective way to tell stories through the environment is by using visual hints. Designers can include small details like worn paths, abandoned buildings, and scattered items to suggest the history and culture of the game world. For example, an old, crumbling castle might hint at a once-great kingdom, while a busy marketplace filled with diverse characters suggests a lively community. These elements add depth and continuity, prompting players to explore and learn more about the world's background.

Additionally, the use of intelligent systems in character interactions boosts the storytelling potential of open worlds. Well-designed non-playable characters (NPCs) can react to players in realistic ways based on what's happening around them. For instance, if an NPC sees the result of a player's actions, like a battle, they might show fear or admiration, depending on what the player has done. This dynamic not only provides immediate feedback but also enriches the storytelling experience, as players can see the effects of their choices reflected in the world and its characters. This interaction fosters a sense of involvement, making players feel more connected to the story.

Furthermore, engaging players on an emotional level is enhanced by including different story paths in gameplay. Designing environments that allow players to make choices that affect the world around them offers a deeper experience. For example, if a player decides to team up with a certain group, it can change the landscape, alter how characters behave, and affect the quests available. When players notice how their decisions shape the game world and its inhabitants, they become more emotionally invested in the story. This creates a more immersive experience, as players observe the consequences of their choices and the world changing in response.

In summary, designing storytelling environments involves a holistic approach that harmonizes visual elements, interactive features, and player choices. Game designers must recognize how each aspect of the environment enhances the storytelling experience. By crafting visually captivating spaces rich in narrative potential, they can create unforgettable experiences that linger in players' minds long after the game concludes. By highlighting the profound connection between the environment, the story, and player decisions, designers can shape open worlds that encourage exploration while delivering powerful and meaningful narratives.

Open World AI Systems and NPC Interactions

The Role of AI in Creating Dynamic Worlds

The use of artificial intelligence (AI) in creating open world games has completely changed how these vast game worlds are built and experienced by players. AI helps design environments that respond and adapt to players' choices, which makes the stories richer and the gaming experience more immersive. Game developers can use AI to create lively worlds where characters that players don't control (known as NPCs) interact with one another and with players, leading to interesting and unique stories that feel real and engaging.

One of the biggest benefits of using AI in these games is the way it allows NPCs to interact in more realistic and meaningful ways. By using advanced technology, game creators can craft characters that behave naturally, react to what players do, and change over time. These interactions can include everything from simple greetings to complex conversations that can affect the game's story. This depth in character behavior enables players to build unique relationships and make choices that have real emotional impact, enhancing the overall gaming experience and giving players a sense of control over the narrative.

AI also plays an important role in making exploration exciting and immersive in open world games. With the help of AI, designers can create varied landscapes and quests that shift based on players' actions and preferences. This encourages players to explore and ensures that each player's adventure feels unique. By incorporating AI-driven storytelling elements, like changing weather or wildlife that reacts to players, designers can immerse players in a world that feels alive and responsive.

Moreover, AI heightens emotional engagement by tracking players' choices and feelings. By observing how players behave and the decisions they make, AI can adapt the game's narrative and gameplay to create personalized experiences. For instance, if a player often helps characters in need, the AI might show that generosity in the game's world, leading to different outcomes and relationships. This connection between players and the story enhances their investment in the game, making their choices feel more significant.

Lastly, AI allows for multiple story paths that cater to different player styles and preferences. Developers can create stories that change based on players' decisions, offering various endings and routes that reflect each player's journey. This not only increases the replayability of games but also lets players explore the moral complexities of their choices. By using AI to manage these intricate storylines, game designers can create worlds that offer not just freedom but also meaningful narratives that stick with players long after they finish the game.

Designing Believable NPC Behaviors

Creating believable characters that players don't control is essential for making open-world games feel real and engaging. These characters, known as non-playable characters (NPCs), play a crucial role in the story and gameplay. How they act and interact with players can greatly affect players' emotional connection to the game. To make these characters believable, game designers need to focus on realism while making sure their actions fit the overall story and respond to the player's choices. This creates a sense of ownership, making players feel that their decisions matter in the game world.

One effective way to design NPC behaviors is by using a mix of planned events and responsive actions. Planned events help guide NPCs to behave in specific ways during important moments in the game. However, to make these characters feel more real, their reactions should also depend on the player's choices and what's happening in the game world. For example, if a player helps an NPC who is in trouble, that character might later offer help or change their attitude based on the player's actions. This dynamic interaction helps the world feel more alive and motivates players to explore and engage since they can see real consequences from their choices.

Another important aspect is giving NPCs emotional depth. These characters should express various feelings that respond to what players do and to the story unfolding around them. By making NPCs exhibit emotions like fear, happiness, or sadness, designers can create characters that players connect with. This emotional depth can come through their dialogue, body language, and voice acting, enriching the storytelling experience. For instance, if a player chooses to betray an NPC, that character might react with anger or disappointment, highlighting the impact of players' decisions.

Additionally, NPCs should have their own distinct personalities and motivations that guide how they behave in the game. This variety allows players to form unique relationships with different characters, enhancing the overall storytelling. By giving NPCs specific goals and backgrounds, designers can create a diverse group that reflects the game's themes. For example, an NPC with a sad history might approach players hesitantly, while a more optimistic character could be eager to interact. This diversity not only deepens the story but also encourages players to explore different options and outcomes based on their interactions.

Lastly, testing and refining NPC behaviors is crucial. Game designers should constantly assess how NPCs engage with players and their environment, gathering feedback on whether they feel believable and engaging. Testing the game can help identify moments where an NPC might seem unrealistic, allowing designers to make improvements to enhance the gaming experience. By continuously testing and refining, designers can ensure that their NPCs not only add to the story but also create a lively and immersive world that players want to explore.

Enhancing Player Interaction with AI

Improving how players interact with characters in open-world video games involves understanding how artificial intelligence (AI) can make these encounters more engaging. Traditionally, many game characters, known as non-player characters (NPCs), react in predictable ways due to pre-written scripts. This can make the interactions feel dull and repetitive. By using smarter AI, game designers can create characters that respond in varied and interesting ways based on what players do, making the game feel more alive and connected.

One effective way to enhance player interaction is by using systems that allow NPCs to react quickly to player choices. For example, depending on how a player has acted in the past—whether they've helped or harmed a character—NPCs can change their responses. This creates a web of relationships that feel realistic and meaningful, adding depth to the overall gaming experience.

Exploration is also key to engaging with these AI-driven characters. Designers can create environments that encourage players to talk with NPCs, leading to different story paths and outcomes. For instance, quests might require players to seek help from characters or gather information, resulting in a variety of emotional stakes and consequences. As players explore and engage with the characters, they become a crucial part of the story, making their choices feel important.

The emotional connection between players and NPCs can be profoundly enriched when these characters exhibit genuine human-like emotions. By endowing NPCs with a spectrum of feelings that shift based on player interactions, games transform into immersive experiences. Imagine an NPC expressing gratitude, suspicion, or fear in response to player actions, reflecting the nuances of real-life social connections. This emotional authenticity invites players to reflect deeply on their choices and the consequences they have on the story and its characters.

Moreover, multi-path storylines reach new heights through the brilliance of intelligent AI. Empowering players to choose varied paths in the narrative, with AI adjusting the storyline based on those choices, greatly enhances replay value. This sparks a sense of adventure, prompting players to explore diverse approaches and yielding unique experiences each time. By weaving AI into the storytelling fabric, game designers can craft richly layered worlds that inspire players to shape their own journeys and outcomes.

Exploration Mechanics that Enhance Storytelling

Designing Compelling Exploration Systems

Creating exciting exploration systems is an essential part of making open world games that balance player freedom with strong storytelling. A good exploration system encourages players to wander around and discover new things while also integrating story elements into the game world. Designers should focus on building environments that spark curiosity and reward players for exploring, making sure they feel in control as they move through the story. This can be done by using visual clues, special items, and changes in the surroundings to hint at a bigger story, allowing players to uncover it at their own pace. It's also important to include smart characters (NPCs) that can make interactions more interesting within these exploration systems. These characters can act as guides, provide quests, or even serve as challenges, all of which add to the game's story. Designers should aim to create NPCs that respond to player actions in real time, making each encounter feel unique and significant. For example, changing what characters say based on player choices or their reactions to how players explore can enhance the experience, helping players connect more deeply with the game world and its characters.

Exploration mechanics should also enrich the storytelling experience. Traditional methods, like collectibles and hidden areas, can be revamped to offer deeper connections to the story. Instead of just giving players items, these features can reveal backstories of characters, historical details, or themes that resonate with the player's journey. Designers should think about how exploration tools, such as maps or compasses, can be linked to the narrative, encouraging players to uncover new aspects of the story as they explore the game world. This connection between gameplay and story ensures that exploration feels meaningful.

Emotional engagement is key when players make choices during their exploration. Players should feel that their decisions matter, influencing both the gameplay experience and the overall story. For example, stumbling upon a hidden village could unlock a special storyline that diverges from the main quest, allowing players to experience the game in a unique way. These systems motivate players to explore thoroughly, deepening their investment in both the story and its emotional stakes.

Lastly, having multiple story paths in a nonlinear game adds depth to exploration. By letting players engage with the story from different angles, designers can create a rich array of narrative experiences that cater to individual preferences. This means offering varied quest lines and making sure exploration rewards align with players' choices throughout the game. Implementing branching dialogues, multiple endings, and different character interactions based on exploration can significantly enhance replayability and depth. Overall, a well-designed exploration system should empower players to shape their own stories, providing a more immersive and engaging open world experience.

Rewards for Exploration: Enhancing the Narrative

Rewards for exploring open world games are crucial for making the story more interesting and keeping players engaged. When designers give players incentives to roam around the expansive landscapes and uncover the intricate plots within these games, it creates a more immersive experience. This not only keeps players hooked but also encourages them to connect more deeply with the story. Rewards can come in different forms, like unique items, bits of background information, or interactions with characters—all of which enhance the storytelling.

One effective way to make exploration more meaningful is through environmental storytelling. Designers can place clues, artifacts, and visual hints throughout the game world that shed light on the background of the story, character histories, or past events. When players find these elements, they gain rewards and piece together the narrative, which fosters a sense of discovery and emotional investment. This approach transforms exploration from a simple activity into a meaningful adventure that enriches the overall story.

Adding dynamic AI for non-player characters (NPCs)

can also significantly enhance how exploration rewards the narrative. When players talk to NPCs, the responses can change based on what the player has done or discovered earlier. This creates a vibrant world where player choices genuinely affect the story, leading to new friendships or story branches. Such systems deepen player engagement and encourage multiple playthroughs, as players look to uncover different interactions and storylines based on their exploration.

The way exploration is designed can further enrich the storytelling experience. Allowing players to choose their own paths, such as through branching quests or optional challenges, gives them a sense of control. When players are rewarded for taking the time to explore and engage with the world, it makes their choices feel valid and meaningful. For example, finding a hidden quest that unlocks crucial plot points can make exploration seem important and necessary to understanding the larger story, rather than just a side activity.

Finally, emotional engagement from players can be enhanced through well-crafted storylines that branch out based on exploration. When players can choose their paths, they become more invested in the results of their decisions. This investment grows when exploration leads to tough choices or significant shifts in the story, making each decision feel important. By connecting exploration with meaningful storytelling, designers can create a rich experience that captivates players and encourages them to explore every aspect of the open world, ultimately enhancing the overall narrative.

Environmental Storytelling Techniques

Environmental storytelling is an exciting way to create deeper narratives in open-world video games. Instead of only using dialogue or cutscenes to share a story, game designers can use the game world itself to tell tales. This technique makes the game more immersive, encouraging players to explore their surroundings and discover hidden stories within the environment. By piecing together clues found in the world, players can learn about its history and feel more connected to the experience.

One popular method of environmental storytelling is through visual details that give context and background. Game designers may include objects, buildings, and scenery that suggest what has happened in a location or hint at the cultures that once lived there. For example, a deserted village might show signs of the lives once lived there, like broken homes and wild gardens. These kinds of details enrich the world and encourage players to dig deeper, making the exploration feel rewarding.

Sound also plays a crucial role in this kind of storytelling. Background sounds, like voices or nature, can help create the atmosphere, while specific sounds can signal important story moments. For instance, if a bustling market suddenly goes silent, it can make players feel a sense of loss or emptiness. Music can heighten emotional moments, helping players feel more involved in the choices they make in the game.

Another powerful way to tell a story through the environment is by changing it based on the player's decisions. When a game responds to what a player does, it creates a world that feels alive and dynamic. As players see how their choices affect the environment, it reinforces the idea of freedom within the game. This encourages them to explore different paths and outcomes, making the story more engaging and helping them feel a stronger connection to the game.

In summary, environmental storytelling is essential for crafting open-world games that focus on a rich narrative and player involvement. By creating environments that tell stories and inspiring players to explore and interact, game designers can develop experiences that are not only entertaining but also emotionally impactful. As the gaming industry grows, using these storytelling techniques will be key to making open-world games that encourage players to think about their choices and the stories they uncover.

Emotional Player Engagement through Open World Choices

Understanding Player Psychology and Engagement

Understanding player psychology is essential for game designers, particularly when creating open-world games that balance freedom and narrative depth. Players engage with games not only through mechanics but also through their emotional and cognitive responses to the virtual worlds they explore. By recognizing how players think and feel, designers can craft experiences that resonate more deeply, leading to greater engagement and satisfaction. Insights into the motivations behind player choices, their emotional investment in characters, and their desire for exploration can significantly inform design decisions.

Exploration mechanics are a vital component of open-world games and play a crucial role in storytelling. Players often seek autonomy and a sense of agency when navigating vast environments. Designers can tap into this desire by creating spaces that reward curiosity and exploration. Incorporating dynamic environmental storytelling, hidden narratives, and interactive elements can encourage players to delve deeper into the game world. When players uncover lore or character backstories through exploration, they gain insights into the game's narrative and forge a more substantial connection to the world and its inhabitants.

Multi-path storylines are also essential for enhancing nonlinear gameplay, as they cater to diverse player preferences and encourage replayability. By providing players with meaningful choices that lead to different outcomes, designers can create a sense of ownership over the narrative. Each decision should have clear consequences that resonate emotionally with players, reinforcing their investment in the story. This approach not only enriches the gameplay experience but also allows players to express their identities through the choices they make, further increasing their engagement with the game.

Integrating AI systems for NPC interactions adds another layer of depth to player engagement. Well-designed

NPCs can reflect the player's choices and react in ways that mirror the complexities of human behavior. This creates a more immersive and believable world where players feel their actions carry weight and significance. Advanced AI can enable dynamic dialogues and adaptive responses that evolve based on the player's decisions, fostering a sense of realism and emotional connection to the game's characters.

Ultimately, fostering emotional player engagement through open-world choices involves creating a balanced interplay between freedom and narrative depth. Players should feel that their actions matter, leading to emotional highs and lows as they navigate the game's landscape. By understanding player psychology and incorporating elements that enhance exploration, storytelling, and character interaction, designers can create rich, engaging experiences that resonate long after gameplay ends. This holistic approach captivates players and encourages them to explore the myriad possibilities within the game world, reinforcing the core principles of freedom and narrative depth in open-world design.

Crafting Choices that Impact Player Experience

Creating choices that truly affect how players experience a game is a key part of designing open world games. Players don't just interact with games through their mechanics; they also connect with the stories that reflect their feelings, fears, and hopes. By making choices meaningful and impactful on the story, developers can build a stronger emotional bond between players and the game world. This connection becomes even more important in open world games, which can sometimes feel overwhelming and distant if not designed carefully.

To ensure players feel their choices matter, game designers need to create a solid structure for these decisions. This means not only having different paths the story can take but also making sure players sense the consequences of their actions. Each choice should lead to changes in character relationships, quest outcomes, and even the game environment. This approach not only gives players a sense of control but also encourages them to explore the game further, as they might want to discover how different decisions can lead to unique results. When players can see how their choices affect the game over time, it deepens the story and motivates them to play again.

Another important aspect is how characters (NPCs) in the game respond to player choices. Using smart systems to create realistic interactions makes the game feel more alive. NPCs should react in ways that reflect the player's actions and decisions. By giving these characters their own personalities and motivations, developers can create a world that feels interactive. For example, if a player decides to betray a character, the resulting tension and changed interactions can significantly influence future quests and the player's overall journey. These kinds of experiences help players feel more connected and invested in the story.

Exploration is also a vital part of storytelling in open world games. Designers should build environments that inspire players to discover stories naturally, whether through the surroundings, hidden lore, or interactions with characters. By weaving narrative elements into the exploration, players can engage with the story at their own pace, making discoveries that feel personal. This enhances the gaming experience while staying true to the open world idea of freedom and choice, allowing players to create their own unique narratives.

Lastly, the emotional impact of choices is crucial in open world design. Players should not only grasp how their decisions work but also feel the emotional weight behind them. By introducing themes like sacrifice, loyalty, or moral dilemmas into the decision-making, designers can evoke strong feelings, making those choices more significant. Storylines that explore different emotional outcomes encourage players to think about their decisions and what they mean, ultimately leading to a more satisfying gameplay experience. In this way, crafting emotionally resonant choices can turn a player's journey into an unforgettable narrative adventure.

Balancing Freedom and Consequence in Decision Making

When it comes to creating open world games, striking the right balance between player freedom and the consequences of their choices is key to making the game enjoyable and memorable. Players love having the freedom to roam around, interact with characters, and make decisions that impact their journey in the game. However, it's important that these choices come with real consequences, so players feel that their decisions matter. Without meaningful outcomes, the game can lose its emotional impact and become less engaging.

One effective way to achieve this balance is through a branching storyline. This means creating multiple paths for players to take based on their choices, leading to different results. Each decision should not only change what happens in the moment but also affect the game's world and its characters in the long run. This gives players a reason to care about the story and encourages them to try out different choices in their gameplay, which enhances replay value. It's crucial that each story branch feels genuine and not just an illusion of choice; this way, players know their actions have real weight.

Another way to enhance this balance is by using smart technology for how non-player characters (NPCs) interact with players. NPCs should react in ways that make sense based on their personalities and motivations, creating a believable world that reacts to the player's actions. For example, if a player decides to betray a character, that character might become hostile, changing how they interact in future situations. This back-and-forth between players and NPCs can deepen emotional connections and reinforce the idea that with freedom comes responsibility.

Exploration is also an important part of how players engage with the game world. Designers should create environments that encourage players to explore and uncover stories and secrets that enrich their understanding of the game. However, exploring should come with the risk of consequences, making it clear that satisfying curiosity can lead to both rewards and unexpected challenges. By weaving these elements into the game's narrative, designers can create a rich and interconnected experience.

Game designers face the inspiring challenge of finding the perfect balance between granting players freedom and ensuring their choices lead to meaningful outcomes. By empowering players to shape their own journeys while ensuring those choices carry significant weight, designers can craft open world games that are not only enjoyable but also deeply emotionally resonant. This balance fosters a profound connection to the game world, encouraging players to reflect on their choices and their significance within the story. As open world games continue to evolve, maintaining this harmony between freedom and consequence is vital for creating truly impactful and engaging experiences.

Multi-Path Storylines in Nonlinear Gameplay
Designing Branching Narratives

Creating engaging stories in open-world video games is all about finding the right balance between letting players make their own choices and keeping the story coherent. The goal is to build a world that feels alive and responsive, allowing players to explore different paths while still being part of a larger narrative. This starts with a strong background story and well-developed characters that can change based on player decisions. Game designers need to think about how each choice affects the game world and its characters, ensuring that the different storylines feel important and not just random.

To make this work, designers can use advanced technology to make game characters react to player actions in real-time. For example, if a player decides to join one group, characters from rival groups might show hostility, while friends could offer special quests or storylines. This level of interaction not only makes the story more interesting but also encourages players to explore different areas to see the results of their decisions.

Exploration is key when it comes to storytelling in open-world games. Designers should weave narrative elements into the game environment itself, using things like hidden objects, abandoned places, or even street art to provide background information and insights into the characters and their histories. By placing these details in the world, players will be motivated to engage with what's around them, uncovering stories that may not be obvious at first. This approach emphasizes that exploring isn't just about getting to a specific place but also about discovering layers of narrative.

Emotional connection is crucial for effective storytelling. Game designers should aim to create choices that resonate with players on a personal level, prompting them to think about their values and decisions. This can be done through stories focused on characters, allowing players to build emotional bonds with the game's figures. By presenting dilemmas that challenge players' morals or beliefs, designers can elicit genuine emotional reactions. The consequences of these choices should be clear and meaningful, affecting the game in a way that reinforces the player's role in shaping the story.

Finally, creating stories that can branch off in different directions presents both challenges and opportunities for designers. It requires careful thought to ensure that all paths feel rewarding and interesting. Each route should offer a unique view of the overall story, giving players different experiences that encourage them to play again. Designers also need to guide players through these various story paths without forcing them into a straight line. Subtle hints—like choices in dialogue, clues in the environment, or character behaviors—can help navigate players while still giving them freedom. Striking this balance between guidance and choice is essential for crafting a rich, interactive storytelling experience in open-world games.

Managing Complexity in Multi-Path Storylines

Creating an engaging open world game involves managing complex storylines that allow players to make choices while still delivering a compelling narrative. Game designers face the challenge of balancing the freedom players crave with a storyline that makes sense and evokes emotions. A well-crafted story with multiple paths lets players explore different adventures while ensuring everything ties together in a satisfying way. This makes players feel more involved in the game world and gives real significance to their decisions.

To handle this complexity effectively, designers need to make sure that players understand the choices they face. Each decision should come with clear consequences so players can see how their actions will impact the story. This can be done with visual hints, dialogue choices, or clues in the environment that suggest what might happen next. However, it's also important to keep an element of surprise; players should feel that their choices lead to unexpected consequences that still make sense. This mix keeps players interested and encourages them to try different paths since they understand the stakes of their decisions.

Another important factor is the role of non-playable characters (NPCs) in the game. Smart NPCs can make the story richer by responding to what players do, creating a lively world that feels alive and reactive. Designers should focus on giving these characters distinct behaviors based on the player's past choices, enhancing the emotional impact of the player's actions and making the game feel more dynamic.

Exploration is also key in a multi-path storyline. Designers can create game environments that motivate players to discover new stories through exploring the world. Secret areas, optional quests, and elements in the environment can encourage players to dig deeper into the game. By rewarding exploration with interesting story elements, designers can enhance the overall experience and create a sense of immersion that encourages players to invest time in uncovering the layers of the plot.

Lastly, it's crucial for designers to think about how players' decisions connect to the bigger picture of the game. Each path should not only influence the immediate story but also resonate with the broader themes and emotions presented in the game. This can be done by developing characters, presenting moral dilemmas, and showing the lasting effects of player choices, even after the game ends. By weaving these aspects into the multi-path storyline, designers can create a rich experience that leaves a lasting impression on players, fostering a deeper emotional connection to the game and its characters.

Tools and Techniques for Nonlinear Storytelling

Nonlinear storytelling in open-world games creates exciting and varied narratives that can greatly increase player involvement. Game designers have the task of exploring different methods to allow players to choose their own paths through the story. A key technique is the branching narrative structure, which involves creating different paths and endings based on the choices players make. To do this well, designers need to carefully plan out potential storylines, ensuring that every choice has real consequences that affect the game world.

Another important aspect is the use of smart dialogue systems for non-player characters (NPCs). These systems enable characters to respond to what players do and say in real time, making interactions feel more realistic and personalized. By using advanced technology that understands language, designers can create conversations that feel natural and are relevant to the player's actions. This not only makes the characters more believable but also encourages players to interact with them on a deeper level, influencing the story based on how they engage.

Exploration is also crucial for nonlinear storytelling. Designers should build immersive environments that spark curiosity and reward players for exploring. This can be done through environmental storytelling, where the game world itself reveals important details about the story and its background. As players explore, they can uncover secrets and complete side quests that deepen their understanding of the game's narrative. Adding puzzles related to the environment can also challenge players to think creatively, further connecting gameplay with storytelling.

Emotional engagement is essential in these types of stories. Designers can create emotional depth through challenging decisions and character development. By placing players in situations where their choices impact the story and the characters' lives, designers help players form a stronger connection with the narrative. This emotional investment encourages players to make choices that align with their own values, leading to a more personalized experience.

Ultimately, weaving together multiple storylines demands a delicate balance of pacing and player agency.

Designers must ensure that, while players are presented with a plethora of choices, the narrative remains cohesive and captivating. Actively seeking feedback from players can shed light on which paths resonate with them, allowing designers to refine these story arcs. This continuous cycle of improvement not only enhances the storytelling but also empowers players, making them feel that their decisions significantly shape the overarching narrative. The result? A richer and more immersive open-world experience that keeps players coming back for more.

The Infinite-Curiosity Approach (ACA)

The challenge of balancing player freedom with narrative progression

Balancing player freedom with a strong storyline is a key challenge in designing open world video games. Game creators need to build worlds that allow players to wander and interact in various ways while making sure the main story stays clear and engaging. Today's players want the freedom to shape their experiences meaningfully, but too much freedom can sometimes lead to stories that feel scattered and less emotionally impactful.

One big hurdle is creating stories with different paths based on player choices without losing the story's essence. Designers need to think about how to develop these paths so they feel natural and connected. This way, players can explore different parts of the story without losing the overall flow. It requires careful planning of the characters and their journeys, ensuring that each decision not only meets the player's interests but also ties back to the main themes and emotions of the game.

Exploration is another important aspect of this balance. Game designers must create environments that spark curiosity and discovery while providing hints and context to help guide players through the story. This can be done through environmental storytelling—the way the setting reveals key parts of the plot or character backgrounds—and responsive interactions with non-playable characters (NPCs) that change based on player choices. Good exploration mechanics should enrich the experience, allowing players to uncover different layers of the story at their own pace without overshadowing critical moments.

Emotional engagement is also crucial for players to connect with the narrative. Designers can encourage this by including meaningful choices that resonate personally with players. These choices should influence gameplay and make players think about their morals and values, deepening their involvement in the story. By using multiple story paths, designers can create experiences that reflect players' unique journeys, ensuring that their freedom enhances the emotional depth of the narrative.

In the end, finding the right balance between player freedom and story progression requires ongoing refinement in design. Game creators should be open to testing and improving their ideas based on player feedback to understand how choice affects their connection to the story. By focusing on a cohesive narrative while embracing the unpredictability of player decisions, designers can create open world games that provide rich, immersive experiences where freedom and storytelling blend seamlessly into an exciting adventure.

Importance of player autonomy in exploration

Player autonomy in exploration is a key part of open world games, which greatly affects how we play and experience stories. When players have the freedom to roam around without strict limitations, they often become more engaged with the game world and its tales. This sense of control allows players to shape their own adventures, making each journey unique based on their choices and preferences. Game designers need to find the right balance between giving players freedom and providing important story elements, ensuring that exploring feels rewarding and meaningful.

In open world games, having this freedom lets players feel more connected to the story. When they can choose their own paths and decide how to interact with the plot, they become co-authors of the narrative. This involvement leads to a stronger emotional connection because players feel that their choices matter and can change the story's outcome. Designers should create exploration opportunities that let players discover background stories and lore naturally, rather than being fed this information in a straightforward way. When players find stories as they explore, it feels more authentic and rewarding.

Additionally, this freedom enhances emotional involvement by allowing players to make choices that resonate with them personally. When they can explore different places and talk to characters at their own pace, they are more likely to bond with those characters and the game world. This emotional connection is crucial for creating unforgettable experiences. Designers can use smart technology to make interactions with characters more dynamic, responding to how players explore, which enriches the story and makes the world feel vibrant. These interactions can lead to surprising story twists, highlighting the value of exploration driven by the player.

Multi-path storylines thrive on player freedom, as they allow for non-linear gameplay that encourages exploration and trying new things. When players can travel to various parts of the game world and encounter different storylines, they're more likely to revisit places and experiment with different choices. This not only increases replay value but also deepens their understanding of the game's world and narratives. Designers should create various paths that reflect the players' choices during their exploration, ensuring that each decision has real consequences that enhance the overall experience.

In the end, prioritizing player freedom in exploration is crucial for designing open world games that resonate with players on many levels. By allowing for movement and choice, designers can create immersive worlds where players feel empowered to tell their own stories. This leads to a more engaging gameplay experience and fosters a stronger connection to the game's narrative and characters. As the gaming industry continues to evolve, embracing player autonomy should be a fundamental principle, ensuring that exploration remains an important and enriching part of open world game design.

The dilemma of providing direction without making players feel guilty for diverging

Creating an open-world video game is a tricky task because designers want players to feel free to explore while still guiding them through a meaningful story. The challenge lies in providing a sense of direction without making players feel bad for choosing different paths. Open worlds are meant to be free and inviting, but balancing that freedom with a compelling narrative takes careful thought.

One effective way to achieve this is by embedding story elements throughout the game environment. By designing rich and immersive worlds filled with hints of history and subtle clues, designers can stimulate players' curiosity. For example, if players come across ancient ruins or mysterious artifacts, it encourages them to investigate and learn more about the game's backstory. This way, players can enjoy the thrill of discovery, all while staying connected to the main story.

Interactions with non-playable characters (NPCs) are also important. Game designers can create NPCs that respond in different ways based on the choices players make. When characters in the game acknowledge players' actions through dialogue or changes in behavior, it makes players feel that their decisions matter, even if they are straying from the main quest. This adds emotional depth to the game and reassures players that exploring other options can enhance their overall experience.

Another strategy is to include multiple story paths. By designing different narrative routes that connect to one another, players can feel more comfortable exploring various choices without fear of missing out on key story elements. When players realize that their decisions can lead to unique but equally satisfying outcomes, they are more likely to embrace their freedom. This not only encourages exploration but also makes players want to replay the game to see all the different possibilities.

Ultimately, the goal is to cultivate a spirit of exploration. By creating open-world games that celebrate player choices, designers can weave narratives that are both vast and cohesive. Allowing players to engage with the game at their own pace while providing gentle guidance through well-placed story elements and responsive NPCs can create a richly rewarding experience. This approach ensures that players feel empowered to explore freely, turning their adventure into a personal journey rather than something they feel obligated to complete.

Differentiating between major and minor landmarks

In open world games, it's important to understand the difference between major and minor landmarks to create an engaging player experience. Major landmarks are the big, important places that players need to notice. These could be famous buildings, key locations tied to the game's story, or spots where important events happen. They help players feel grounded in the game world and guide them through the storyline, making the game more exciting and emotionally engaging.

On the other hand, minor landmarks add charm and detail to the game environment, even if they're not central to the main plot. These can include interesting rock formations, quaint little buildings, or secret spots waiting to be discovered. While they may not affect the main story directly, they make the world feel richer and encourage players to explore. By including these smaller features, designers create a more vivid and believable world that invites players to look deeper.

The relationship between major and minor landmarks can also enhance storytelling in a game. Major landmarks draw players in, while minor ones provide extra context that makes the story feel more complete. For example, if you find a little shrine next to a big, important castle, it might reveal something intriguing about the game's history or culture. This layered storytelling allows players to connect with the plot on different levels, rewarding those who explore.

Additionally, where and how these landmarks are placed can influence how players behave and make choices. Major landmarks might be positioned where they can be seen from far away, building excitement and purpose. In contrast, minor landmarks might be hidden in less obvious spots, encouraging players to wander off the main path. This setup not only promotes exploration but also gives players the freedom to choose how deeply they want to engage with the story and the world.

In the end, understanding the difference between major and minor landmarks is crucial for creating open world games. By thoughtfully integrating both types, designers can build a fascinating environment that balances player freedom with a strong narrative. This balance is key to crafting experiences that truly resonate with players, making them feel connected to the world and its story, leading to memorable moments in gameplay.

Major landmarks tied to critical plot points

In the world of open-world video games, major landmarks play an important role in creating engaging stories and keeping players interested. These landmarks act like significant points of interest that help guide the plot and allow players to form a deeper connection with the game world. Game designers skillfully place these important locations in the gameplay to create a rich mix of stories that unfold as players explore and interact with their surroundings. This relationship between the environment and the story makes the game feel more immersive, helping players feel emotionally invested in the world they're navigating.

One effective way to incorporate these landmarks is through storytelling woven into the design of buildings and landscapes. Designers can include bits of history and background in the structures players come across, allowing them to learn about significant events without lengthy explanations. For instance, a dilapidated castle might tell the tale of a once-prosperous kingdom through its ruins, with non-playable characters (NPCs) sharing stories of what happened. This approach not only provides context but also encourages players to dig deeper and explore the world for clues about the story.

Landmarks also play an important role in guiding players' choices and paths within the game. By placing key objectives or decision points near these landmarks, designers can create moments filled with suspense and excitement. For example, a hidden temple might present players with two different quests to choose from, leading them to different outcomes. These choices give players a sense of control over the story, which is vital in open-world games, making them feel more connected to the narrative.

Additionally, landmarks can enhance interactions with NPCs—characters controlled by the game. By placing NPCs in or near these important locations, designers can make the gameplay richer with dynamic conversations that reflect the players' choices. NPCs might share insights about the landmark's history or respond differently based on what players have done before. This kind of interaction not only adds depth to the story but also encourages players to return to these landmarks, creating a cycle of exploration and discovery that keeps the game exciting.

In summary, the careful placement and design of major landmarks in open-world games can greatly impact how stories are told. By using these locations as storytelling tools, designers can enhance exploration, foster emotional connections, and offer a variety of story paths that cater to player choices. As game designers continue to push boundaries in this genre, understanding the significance of these landmarks will be vital in crafting immersive worlds that invite players to explore not just the landscape, but the very narratives within them.

Filling intervening spaces with engaging content

Filling in the gaps between major events in an open-world game is essential for creating a captivating experience for players. Instead of treating these areas as just empty spaces, game designers can transform them into opportunities for storytelling. By adding interesting interactions, environmental details, and lively non-playable characters (NPCs), designers can keep players engaged and deepen their connection to the game's story.

One effective way to tell a story in these spaces is through environmental storytelling. This means using the game's setting—like buildings, objects, and landscapes—to hint at the world's history and culture without having to explain everything outright. For example, observing remnants of past battles or ancient artifacts can spark curiosity about the game's backstory. These elements invite players to explore and learn about the world simply by wandering through it, making every step of the journey meaningful.

Dynamic NPCs also play a big role in making these spaces lively and engaging. When NPCs interact with players—through conversations, sharing gossip, or reacting to players' choices—it creates a sense of a vibrant world. This interaction can lead players to side quests or hidden stories, making the world feel more alive and immersive. By giving NPCs different responses based on player actions, designers enhance the feeling that decisions matter in the game, reinforcing the overall themes and emotional stakes.

Exploration is another key aspect. Game designers can add puzzles, secret paths, and collectibles that reward players for being curious. These features should tie into the story, so that even small side quests can reveal important information about the plot or characters. When exploration feels rewarding, players are more likely to venture off the main path and enjoy surprises that deepen their emotional investment in the game.

Ultimately, the aim is to create a smooth storytelling experience that respects players' choices while enhancing their emotional connection to the game. By allowing for multiple story paths in these spaces, players can make decisions that shape the story's direction. This approach not only empowers them but also inspires them to care about the world and its characters. By recognizing the storytelling potential in these areas, game designers can build expansive worlds filled with captivating stories just waiting to be discovered.

Resources that incentivize exploration

In the world of open world games, finding exciting things to discover plays a big part in how players enjoy their experience. These rewards can come in many forms, like items to collect, intriguing stories, or interesting interactions with characters in the game. By placing these incentives in various parts of the game, designers can encourage players to explore beyond the usual paths, sparking curiosity and excitement that enriches the overall story.

One way to encourage exploration is through collectibles, such as ancient artifacts or journal pages, which can reveal important background information about the game's story and characters. When players find these items scattered throughout the game, it creates a sense of mystery, inviting them to uncover the history of the world they are in. Each new discovery not only rewards their curiosity but also deepens their emotional connection to the characters and the overall narrative.

Another engaging element is how characters in the game react to players' exploration. For example, if a player finds a hidden area, non-player characters (NPCs) might acknowledge this by mentioning the player's discovery in their conversations or offering quests related to it. This interaction makes the game feel more alive, showing players that their actions have real consequences and motivating them to engage more with the game world.

The environment itself can also tell stories without using words. By designing beautiful and detailed surroundings that hint at the game's narrative, players are encouraged to pay attention and explore. Details like old ruins, signs of past battles, or the arrangement of plants and animals can all suggest untold stories. This allows players to interpret the game world in their own way, creating a personal and rewarding experience.

Finally, allowing for different paths and outcomes based on exploration can greatly enrich the player experience. When quests or storylines change depending on where players choose to go, it creates a sense of freedom and control. This encourages players to discover various areas of the game world and increases replayability, as they might want to explore all the different possibilities. By weaving these engaging elements into the game design, developers can create a vibrant world that players want to explore, enhancing the depth of the story and overall experience.

Avoiding mandates for progression

When it comes to designing open world video games, one of

the most important things to think about is how to let players progress without forcing them to follow strict rules. Allowing players the freedom to choose their path creates a much more enjoyable experience. This way, players can explore the game world and connect with the story at their own pace. Instead of feeling like they have to go down a specific road, players can stumble upon story elements naturally, making their experience more immersive and emotionally engaging.

To help with this, game designers should focus on creating environments that offer a lot of choices. This means designing worlds full of opportunities for players to interact with various quests and characters whenever they want. By having multiple ways to engage with the story, players can customize their experience based on what they enjoy most, whether that's fighting enemies, exploring the environment, or chatting with other characters. This flexibility makes the gameplay much more enjoyable and helps players form a stronger connection to the story and its characters.

Adding smart systems that allow the game characters—NPCs—to react to player decisions can further enhance this sense of freedom. If players see that their choices really impact the game world and its inhabitants, they're more likely to dive deeper into the story. This creates a vibrant world where actions have consequences, encouraging players to explore different paths and see various outcomes without feeling confined by set goals.

Additionally, exploring the game can be designed in a way that rewards those who stray from the main story. Side quests, hidden locations, and storytelling through the game environment can entice players to wander off the main path. By weaving interesting narrative elements into exploration, designers create a rich world of stories that players can uncover on their own terms. This not only cultivates a spirit of discovery but also allows players to shape their own narrative based on the choices they make throughout the game.

In the end, allowing players the freedom to choose their own progression creates a gaming environment where they feel empowered to follow their own paths. This freedom leads to a deeper engagement with the game's story, as players actively participate in shaping what happens rather than just following instructions. Thoughtfully designed open world games can go beyond traditional storytelling, offering players a personal experience that leaves a lasting impression long after they finish the game. By adopting this approach, game designers can create worlds that celebrate exploration and choice, inviting players to fully immerse themselves in the stories they create.

Benefits of exploring landmarks

Exploring notable places in open world games is an essential part of making the player experience richer and more engaging. These landmarks can be anything from impressive buildings to hidden ancient sites, each offering unique visuals and themes that capture players' interest. When game creators thoughtfully design these points of attraction, they help build a lively and immersive environment. Players are naturally inclined to visit these memorable locations, which can serve as important storytelling anchors, guiding them through the game's intricate plot while encouraging them to explore and discover more.

One of the main advantages of including landmarks is their ability to enhance the story as players explore. Game developers can strategically place these landmarks to lead players to important moments in the narrative or details about the characters. For example, a crumbling castle might tell the tragic tale of a lost kingdom, while a bustling marketplace could introduce players to important non-playable characters (NPCs) who give out quests or key information. By creating these focal points, designers can make the act of exploring feel purposeful and rewarding, prompting players to engage more deeply with the game world.

Moreover, landmarks can really affect how players emotionally connect with the game through their choices. When players come across a landmark, they often find themselves thinking about what it symbolizes in the story. For instance, a memorial site might trigger feelings of loss and nostalgia, which can influence how players make decisions later on. This emotional connection not only deepens the player's relationship with the storyline but also gives them a sense of control,

allowing them to shape their journey based on their feelings towards these significant places. So, landmarks act as powerful tools for storytelling, making players feel more invested in the game.

Additionally, landmarks are crucial for branching storylines in games that allow for nonlinear play. By providing different paths to explore, game designers can create various narrative outcomes based on players' choices at these sites. For example, if a player decides to confront a villain at a famous landmark, the story's conclusion may differ from if they had chosen to gather support at a nearby tavern. This variety not only encourages players to replay the game but also empowers them to create their unique stories, making each playthrough a different experience.

Lastly, the layout of landmarks can improve interactions with NPCs, which is a key element in open world games. Well-placed landmarks can act as spots where players meet characters, leading to natural conversations and quest opportunities that feel integral to the world. This can result in more meaningful relationships between players and NPCs, as encounters at these significant places can reveal deeper motivations or secrets about the characters. By connecting landmarks with how NPCs behave, designers can weave a rich tapestry of interactions that pull players further into the story and inspire them to explore the game's themes more thoroughly.

Enhancements (health, stamina)

In the world of open world games, how health and stamina work is really important for making the game enjoyable and engaging. These features are not just about keeping your character alive; they also help players feel more connected to the story of the game. When game designers create systems for health and stamina, they can encourage players to make smart choices that affect their journey through the game. This means players can explore the game world more deeply while managing their resources, which makes the gameplay and story feel more connected.

Health systems can show the consequences of players' choices, making the game even more exciting. For example, in a game where health is linked to moral decisions, players might discover that their actions can affect their character's well-being and their relationships with other characters in the game. This adds an emotional layer, as players need to think about the risks of their decisions and how they might be rewarded in the story. When health influences the narrative, players become more invested in the character's journey and the overall story.

Stamina systems also play a key role in exploration and storytelling. By adding a stamina meter that controls things like running, climbing, or interacting with the environment, designers can create feelings of urgency and challenge. Players need to manage their stamina while navigating large game worlds, which leads to important decision-making. This can add tension to the game, encouraging players to think about what happens if they push themselves too hard, like running into enemies or missing important story moments. In this way, stamina not only affects gameplay but also enhances the story.

Additionally, both health and stamina systems can be improved with various upgrades that players can find or earn in the game. These upgrades might give players temporary boosts, permanent enhancements, or unique items that change how health and stamina work. By connecting these upgrades to specific parts of the story or character growth, designers can create rich adventures that reward players for exploring and trying new things. For instance, a player might find a special herb that not only helps restore health but also reveals a piece of the game's hidden lore, making the experience even more rewarding.

In conclusion, carefully integrating health and stamina features in open world games makes for a deeper and more engaging experience. By linking these mechanics to the story, game designers can create narratives that resonate emotionally with players, encouraging them to make meaningful choices that impact both their gameplay and the unfolding story. As open world games continue to develop, using these enhancements will be key to creating immersive worlds where freedom and storytelling go hand in hand, leading to a stronger connection between players and the game.

Opportunities for rest and resource gathering

In open-world games, taking breaks and gathering resources are important parts that make the gameplay more enjoyable and meaningful. These activities not only help players collect necessary items for survival and progress but also create moments for reflection and emotional connection. By including opportunities to rest and gather resources, game designers can create a more immersive experience that emphasizes themes of freedom and exploration.

As players journey through the game, resting spots can be strategically located throughout the world. These areas serve as safe places where players can recharge and think about their adventures. Designers can enhance these resting spots with interesting visuals, unique buildings, and relaxing sounds, helping players feel connected to the environment. Some resting moments might also reveal story elements, like character conversations or flashbacks, deepening players' relationships with the storyline and characters. These breaks are crucial for pacing, allowing players to absorb the story and prepare for upcoming challenges.

Gathering resources is just as important, as it keeps the gameplay exciting and builds the world around the player. When players collect items, they aren't just checking off a task; they're enriching the game world. Designers can make this experience more engaging by linking the resources players collect to the game's story. For example, a player could gather healing herbs in a magical forest or mine valuable metals in an ancient mountain. These connections not only support the game's story but also encourage players to explore and interact with their surroundings.

Additionally, involving non-playable characters (NPCs) can add even more meaning to resting and gathering resources. NPCs can give players quests or share interesting stories about the area, making resource collection feel more relevant. By building relationships with these characters, players can feel a sense of community and shared history, enhancing their overall experience. These relationships may change based on the player's choices, leading to unique conversations and quests that reflect their decisions throughout the game.

In summary, resting and resource gathering are more than just game mechanics; they play a crucial role in making the game emotionally engaging and narratively rich. By thoughtfully designing these elements, game developers can create a deeper and more rewarding experience that resonates with players on many levels. This approach not only enhances the player's journey but also encourages them to reflect on their choices, forging a stronger connection to the story and its characters.

Sharing of rumors and lore

In the vast landscapes of open-world games, rumors and lore are the heartbeat of a vibrant narrative, drawing players in with the promise of adventure and discovery. These elements not only enhance world-building but also ignite curiosity, encouraging players to explore every nook and cranny and interact with colorful non-player characters (NPCs). Imagine stumbling upon whispers of a long-lost treasure or tales of legendary heroes that guide you towards quests, deepening your understanding and connection to the game world. By weaving these stories into the game's tapestry, designers create a dynamic ecosystem where players are driven to uncover secrets and piece together the rich history of their surroundings.

To bring rumors and lore to life, it's essential for designers to think about how NPCs share their knowledge. Imagine a dialogue system that adapts to your choices, where each NPC, with their unique quirks and motivations, might offer tantalizing hints about hidden artifacts or enigmatic events. This personalization enhances the experience, allowing players to interact in varied ways that match their play style and fostering a greater sense of agency within the game.

Environmental storytelling also plays a pivotal role, breathing life into every corner of the world. Picture ancient ruins scattered throughout the landscape, each one a puzzle piece containing clues about past conflicts and forgotten heroes.

These details invite players to embark on thorough explorations, rewarding their curiosity with hidden narratives waiting to be unearthed. This layered approach transforms the game into a living entity, where every whisper of lore and every environmental clue is interconnected, enriching players' journeys.

As players delve deeper into these tales, emotional engagement peaks when they encounter lore that resonates with their unique choices. Consider a gripping story about a fallen hero that unfolds into a quest, forcing players to grapple with whether to uphold the hero's legacy or to seek retribution against their betrayers. By allowing player decisions to shape the narrative, designers cultivate a profound connection that compels players to think critically about their actions and the larger implications within the story arc.

Furthermore, the beauty of multi-path storylines intertwines seamlessly with the fabric of rumors and lore. When players encounter a rumor that leads them to a hidden faction, the choices they make could spark alliances or betrayals, culminating in unique outcomes. This branching narrative design bestows players with the freedom to forge their own paths, crafting a personal and memorable journey. Not only does this enhance replayability, but it also elevates players to active participants in an ever-evolving story, where every choice matters and every adventure is their own.

Creating a Loop of Engagement

In open world games, keeping players engaged is crucial for making sure they connect with the game's world and story. This engagement happens through a blend of player choices, exploration, and the impact those choices have on the game. To create a compelling experience, game designers need to ensure that players feel their decisions matter and that exploring the game leads them to discover not just the scenery but also important aspects of the story and its characters. Striking the right balance between allowing freedom and providing direction is key, so players can choose their own adventures while still interacting with the main storyline in meaningful ways.

One effective way to maintain this engagement is by designing characters in the game that respond and change based on what players do. Game worlds can come alive if non-playable characters (NPCs) have conversations and relationships that feel genuine. For example, if a player helps a town, the NPCs might offer special quests or rewards to show their appreciation. On the other hand, if a player takes a destructive approach, the town's reaction might involve hostility or isolation. This kind of responsive interaction not only keeps players engaged with immediate feedback but also makes them think about the wider impact of their choices.

Exploration is also vital for enhancing the game's storytelling. When players are rewarded for finding hidden stories, clues, and character backgrounds, it deepens their connection to the game world. By placing interesting details in unexpected places, designers encourage players to explore every part of the game. This enriches the overall experience and links exploration directly to the story, emphasizing how players' curiosity can lead to greater understanding and emotional investment.

Players feel even more connected when they realize their choices can significantly change how the story unfolds. To create this connection, designers should offer different story paths that change based on what players decide. This might mean that different choices lead to various storylines, each featuring unique characters and challenges. By allowing players to shape the story, they become more engaged in the gameplay, wanting to return and explore different choices and outcomes.

Lastly, incorporating feedback into the gameplay helps deepen this engagement. Designers should consider how players' actions create both immediate and lasting changes in the game, creating a cycle that encourages players to keep interacting. For example, a decision might alter the game world, which then affects future choices players can make. This ongoing relationship between what players do, how it changes the game, and how the story develops not only keeps players interested but also provides a richer, more immersive experience that aligns with the essence of open world games focused on freedom and storytelling depth.

Exploration yielding discoveries

Exploration is a fundamental part of open world video games, allowing players to roam expansive landscapes and discover hidden stories. This section focuses on how exploration can lead to exciting discoveries and how thoughtful game design can enhance players' enjoyment and storytelling experiences. By creating lively environments filled with intriguing backstories, secrets, and things to interact with, designers can spark a sense of wonder and curiosity that invites players to explore more deeply.

To encourage exploration, game creators need to build a rich and varied world. This means designing different regions with unique cultures and histories that players can engage with. Each place should have its own stories and surprises that reward those who are curious. For example, including elements like ancient ruins, hidden treasures, or characters with their own mini-stories can motivate players to investigate their surroundings. This not only offers immediate rewards but also connects the player's journey to the larger story of the game world.

Another important aspect of making exploration enjoyable involves giving characters in the game a level of intelligence. Smart characters can react to what players do, creating a more dynamic world. If these characters can change their responses based on a player's discoveries, it adds depth to their interactions. For instance, a character might give different advice or quests depending on what the player has found. This responsive nature encourages players to explore further and makes the game feel more alive and engaging.

Emotional connection is another key benefit of exploration. When players uncover personal stories or emotional adventures tied to their exploration, it deepens their bond with the game world. Finding an old letter in a deserted house or meeting a ghost tied to a sad event can create moments of empathy and reflection. These instances remind players that exploring isn't just about moving through a game space; it's also about the emotional journeys they experience as they learn more about the story.

Lastly, offering multiple story paths can enhance the

exploration experience. By creating storylines that change based on the player's choices, game developers allow for a rich variety of experiences. This means players can enjoy different outcomes depending on the routes they take while exploring, making every player's journey unique. As players uncover different pieces of the story through exploration, they become co-creators of their adventures, leading to a deeper connection with the game and its characters. In this way, exploration not only leads to discoveries but also transforms playing into a meaningful interaction with the story and the player's choices.

Ensuring players find multiple new items/concepts

In designing open world games, it's important to keep players interested and excited by introducing them to various new items and ideas. One great way to do this is by adding a wide selection of items that not only help players in the game but also enhance the story and the world around them. This could include unique treasures, materials for crafting, or special pieces of lore that players can find as they explore. Each item should have its own story or meaning within the game's universe, which encourages players to investigate their surroundings and connect with the game world on a deeper level.

To make the experience even more engaging, designers can create systems that introduce new items based on how players choose to play. For instance, using smart technology, a game could learn what a player enjoys and then present them with items that match their style. This might include personalized gear that boosts their abilities or special collectibles tied to certain quests. By customizing these discoveries, players enjoy a more personal experience that keeps them eager to explore further.

Additionally, introducing new ways to interact with items can enhance the game. Allowing players to craft, upgrade, or combine items offers opportunities for creativity and experimentation. For example, a simple item can become something more powerful through a player's efforts, creating a sense of ownership and accomplishment. Moreover, enabling players to share or trade items with other characters in the game can encourage social interaction, making the game feel richer and more connected.

Another important factor is the timing of when players find new items. To keep players interested, it's crucial to balance how often and how significant these discoveries are throughout the game. A well-designed progression system can guide players through a carefully structured story, where each new item feels like an important milestone. This approach helps maintain curiosity about what's to come while allowing players to fully appreciate the significance of each new discovery.

Finally, having different story paths can greatly enhance the experience of finding new items. When players can make choices that lead to different outcomes, each playthrough reveals new items and experiences, encouraging them to replay the game. For example, a powerful artifact might appear based on the friendships a player has formed or decisions they've made. This not only makes the story richer but also highlights how important player choices are in shaping their unique adventure. By ensuring players discover a variety of new items and ideas, game designers can create a lively world that feels responsive and engaging, leading to a memorable gaming experience.

Fostering a continuous loop of engagement

Creating an engaging experience in open world games is key to making them feel immersive and captivating for players. This means designing game elements that encourage players to explore the game world while also making them feel connected to the story. A great way to keep players involved is by combining exploration, interactions with characters, and meaningful choices that let players create their own stories. Game designers can bring the world to life and make it responsive to player actions by understanding what motivates players.

Exploration is a fundamental part of open world games. It's how players discover the story. Designers should create environments that reward curiosity, prompting players to explore areas that aren't just part of the main path. This can be done through hidden stories, details in the scenery, and events that change based on what players do. When players find secret information or see the outcomes of their choices, they become more invested in the game, leading to a cycle of continuous exploration.

Interacting with non-playable characters (NPCs) is also very important in enhancing the player's experience and adding depth to the story. By using smarter AI for these characters, designers can create more realistic conversations and interactions. It's essential that NPCs have unique personalities and motivations that react to what the player does. This can create storylines where player choices affect relationships and change the game world. When NPCs are more than just quest-givers and feel like real participants in the story, the game world becomes much more engaging and believable.

Having multiple story paths is another important way to keep players engaged. When players can make choices that genuinely change their experience, it adds excitement. By offering different storylines and endings, game designers can appeal to various player preferences, encouraging them to play the game again. Each choice players make should feel important, making them think about how their actions influence the game world. This not only makes the game more emotionally engaging but also gives players a sense of control over their experience.

Ultimately, the goal is to create a strong emotional bond between the player and the game. By blending a rich story with gameplay, designers can craft moments that resonate on a personal level. This can involve deep character development, tough moral choices, and impactful plots that challenge players' beliefs. When players emotionally connect with the story and characters, they are more likely to become fully engaged with the game, leading to a richer and more rewarding experience. By fostering these connections, designers create a world that players not only want to explore but also feel attached to, keeping their interest alive throughout their journey.

Aligning players' curiosity with narrative progression

Connecting players' curiosity with the story in open-world games is a key ingredient that can make the game more enjoyable and meaningful. In these vast game worlds, players are often driven by a natural desire to explore, discover new things, and interact with everything around them. To make the most of this curiosity, game designers need to weave the story elements into the exploration, offering players worthwhile rewards for their adventures. This can include storytelling through the environment, hidden pieces of lore, and character histories that deepen the game's narrative, allowing players to find out the story at their own pace.

To create an experience where exploration leads to story development, designers must think carefully about how they introduce information. For instance, placing story clues in surprising spots or revealing them through the actions of characters that players can interact with can ignite curiosity and encourage players to dig deeper. This approach not only rewards players for exploring but also gives them a sense of control as they piece the story together through their experiences.

Additionally, emotional engagement grows when players feel their decisions genuinely influence the story. Designers can strengthen this connection by allowing players to make choices that affect relationships and story outcomes. This means having different paths the story can take, which can change based on what players decide, encouraging them to explore different storylines or endings. This design not only makes players want to revisit the game but also raises the emotional stakes.

The use of smart AI for character interactions is also vital in linking curiosity with story progression. When non-playable characters (NPCs) respond realistically to what players do, it enhances the storytelling. For example, an NPC might share special insights or offer unique quests based on previous interactions or discoveries, motivating players to explore even more. This connection helps players feel that their choices matter and adds depth to the game world.

In essence, aligning players' curiosity with storytelling requires a well-rounded approach that includes exploration mechanics, emotional involvement, and intelligent character interactions. By carefully designing these elements, game creators can develop open-world experiences that not only encourage players to explore but also reward their curiosity with rich and meaningful stories. This connection enriches players' overall satisfaction and deepens the narrative quality of the game, crafting a lively world where curiosity and storytelling go hand in hand.

Case Studies

When we look at how open world video games are designed, we see a fascinating connection between storytelling and the freedom players have to explore. A great example of this is "The Witcher 3: Wild Hunt." This game is known for its rich storytelling and vast world, where players can choose their paths and make decisions that significantly impact the story and the game world. It shows that allowing players to make choices can lead to a highly personal experience, making the narrative feel even more engaging.

Another excellent example is "Red Dead Redemption 2." This game dives deep into emotional storytelling, using its beautiful environments and character interactions to draw players in. Characters in the game react to what players do, thanks to smart AI technology. The mix of scripted events and players' actions creates a lively world that feels real, pulling players into the story and making them feel connected to the characters.

"Breath of the Wild" is also worth mentioning for how it encourages exploration. This game lets players wander through its huge world at their own pace, rewarding their curiosity with hidden stories, side quests, and intriguing details found in the environment. This open-ended style of play lets players create their own adventures and shows how exploring can be a big part of storytelling in games.

On the other hand, "Cyberpunk 2077" offers a different look at storytelling with its many different paths. Players can make choices that change the story and how characters relate to one another. However, this complexity can sometimes be challenging, as it's important for all the possible story branches to feel meaningful. This game highlights how tricky it can be to balance player freedom with a clear story.

Finally, "Ghost of Tsushima" demonstrates how culture can enhance storytelling in open world games. Set in feudal Japan, it combines historical elements with personal stories, allowing players to engage with the game's themes of honor and sacrifice. By weaving in cultural and historical contexts, the game creates a rich, immersive experience that resonates with players on different levels.

These examples show that open world games can tell deep, engaging stories while giving players the freedom to explore and make their own choices.

"The Legend of Zelda: Breath of the Wild"

The Legend of Zelda: Breath of the Wild is a groundbreaking game that changed how open world games are made, showing how freedom and storytelling can come together to create a rich experience for players. Set in the large kingdom of Hyrule, the game allows players to wander through a colorful world filled with different landscapes, deep stories, and many quests to embark on. This wide-open world lets players take on challenges in their own ways, focusing on personal exploration and choices rather than following a strict path. Players are encouraged to interact with their environment, leading to exciting discoveries that feel rewarding.

One of the standout features of Breath of the Wild is how it handles interactions with characters in the game. Unlike many games where characters often stick to scripted lines and predictable actions, this game has a system that lets characters respond in ways that feel real based on what players do. This makes the story more engaging, as players can affect what happens through their choices and how they interact with the world around them. The lively AI systems help create an environment that feels alive, making every meeting with a character memorable.

Exploration is a key part of what makes Breath of the Wild special. The game is designed so players can freely climb mountains, glide above the land, and discover new areas, which adds to the sense of adventure. The beautiful landscapes tell their own stories, allowing players to learn about the history of Hyrule as they uncover ancient ruins and hidden challenges. This exploration deepens players' connection to the game world and its rich story.

An important element of Breath of the Wild is the emotional connection it fosters with players. The game encourages players to make choices that reflect their personal feelings. Whether it's deciding to help a struggling village or searching remote areas for secrets, every action carries significance and enhances players' investment in the story. The freedom to approach tasks in any order creates a unique experience, allowing players to engage with themes of bravery, perseverance, and the importance of their choices.

Finally, Breath of the Wild successfully uses a storytelling approach that allows for multiple paths within its flexible gameplay. Players aren't stuck with just one storyline; they can explore various quests and challenges that come together to create a rich overall experience. This design choice gives players the power to discover different parts of the story at their own pace, leading to a variety of interpretations and endings. As a result, the game not only showcases the potential of open world design but also serves as inspiration for other game creators who want to build worlds where freedom and storytelling can live in harmony.

Exploration and narrative integration examples

In open world games, exploration is a key part of how players connect with the story, making the experience feel natural and engaging. A great example of this is "The Legend of Zelda: Breath of the Wild." Here, players can roam through vast landscapes at their own speed, encountering various environmental details that tell the story of Hyrule's history. As players discover ruins, shrines, and hidden treasures, they piece together a larger narrative, making the journey feel meaningful and giving a sense of freedom that defines open world games. Another excellent example is "The Witcher 3: Wild Hunt," which combines exploration with a rich story through its quest system. Instead of following a straight path, players have many quests, encouraging them to explore the world deeply. Side quests often reveal important details about characters and the difficult choices they face, making the players feel more connected to the story and its characters.

Additionally, using advanced AI for interactions with non-player characters (NPCs) can greatly improve the storytelling experience in these games. In "Red Dead Redemption 2," for example, the way NPCs respond is shaped by the player's actions and choices. NPCs remember past interactions, react differently based on the player's reputation, and have conversations that feel realistic. This not only enhances the story but also gives players a sense of impact, making them feel that their actions matter in this living world. Exploration in video games isn't just about reaching a destination; it's about forging emotional connections that linger long after the game ends. Take "Firewatch," for instance. Set against the breathtaking backdrop of the Wyoming wilderness, players step into the shoes of Henry, a fire lookout grappling with personal demons. As he interacts with his supervisor, Delilah, over the radio, players delve deep into his journey and struggles. The stunning natural scenery mirrors Henry's internal conflicts, creating a powerful synergy between gameplay and storytelling that draws players into a profound emotional bond with the character.

Then there's "Cyberpunk 2077," a masterpiece of choice where every exploration leads to new adventures. Set in the vibrant, chaotic world of Night City, players encounter diverse factions, intriguing side missions, and unforgettable characters. Each choice branches into unique storylines, allowing players to chart their own course through the narrative. This ability to shape one's story makes every playthrough feel personal and fresh. By prioritizing exploration as a means of unearthing rich narratives, game designers unlock a world of immersive storytelling potential in open-world games, inviting players to experience the thrill of discovery like never before.

"Elden Ring"

Elden Ring is a fantastic game that showcases how to create a large, open world filled with engaging stories. The game takes place in a place called the Lands Between, which is beautifully designed to encourage players to explore every nook and cranny. As players wander around, they discover intriguing stories, hidden quests, and various pieces of lore that make the experience richer. This thoughtful world design highlights how important it is for games to allow players to interact with their surroundings in ways that make the gameplay and the story feel connected.

One of the great aspects of Elden Ring is its storytelling style. Players can explore the vast landscape at their own pace and encounter different groups and characters, each contributing to a unique storyline. This openness teaches game creators how to implement different paths in storytelling that change based on what players choose, giving them a sense of control that makes the game more engaging. When players can shape their own adventures, they develop stronger connections to the game and its characters, making each choice feel significant.

The game also offers an interesting look at how players interact with non-playable characters (NPCs), those characters who aren't controlled by players. These NPCs are more than just people handing out quests; they are deeply woven into the game's story. They react to what players do and change as the game progresses, leading to a more lively experience. For game makers, creating smart NPCs that respond to player actions can make the game world feel more real. Characters that interact meaningfully with players can enrich the story while giving players a stronger sense of involvement.

Exploring the world in Elden Ring is also central to the storytelling. Players are encouraged to look around and uncover stories hidden in the environment. The game cleverly uses visual cues and items filled with lore to guide players while still allowing for surprises. By intertwining exploration with the story, players can piece together narratives and deepen their emotional connection to the game, making the world feel more alive and interconnected.

In the realm of Elden Ring, players don't just traverse a vast landscape; they embark on an emotionally charged journey defined by the choices they make. Each decision presents a moral dilemma, urging players to ponder not only their next move but also the broader implications of their actions. This nuanced emphasis on choice deepens the connection players feel to the game, transforming their journey into a personal narrative woven with their values and beliefs.

Game designers can draw inspiration from this compelling approach to craft experiences that elevate meaningful interactions and choices to the forefront. By prioritizing emotional engagement and the weight of decision-making, developers can create open-world games that resonate profoundly, leaving players with unforgettable memories and self-reflection long after the game is over.

Case Studies of Successful Open World Games

Analyzing Narrative Techniques of Far Cry

Far Cry is a video game series that tells its stories in unique ways, helping players feel more involved in its vast open worlds. One of the standout techniques is environmental storytelling. This means that the game world itself is designed so that each location hints at a story through its visuals, buildings, and the remains of past events. Players can discover the narrative without needing constant dialogue or cutscenes, which encourages them to explore and engage with the surroundings. Game designers can learn from this by making sure the game world itself tells a story, drawing players in to discover more. Character development is also a crucial part of Far Cry's storytelling. The games present intriguing villains who often represent complex moral questions, pushing players to think about their values and choices. By creating well-rounded characters, the game encourages players to invest emotionally in the story. Designers can take note of this by ensuring that key characters in their own games are not only memorable but also challenge players to reflect on their actions and decisions.

Another important element in Far Cry's design is player agency. Players are given various choices that can change how the story unfolds, leading to multiple endings. This non-linear style caters to players' desires for freedom and encourages them to replay the game. Designers should focus on creating impactful decisions that resonate with players, demonstrating that their choices can shape the storyline. By incorporating different paths, developers can offer a more personalized gaming experience that deepens emotional connections. Interactions with non-player characters (NPCs) also significantly enhance player experiences. In Far Cry, the AI allows these characters to respond to player actions, creating a sense of realism and consequence. This makes the game world feel alive and responsive. For game designers, focusing on advanced AI that supports meaningful interactions can improve storytelling, making players feel that their actions truly matter in the game.

Lastly, exploring the game world is closely related to how the story unfolds in Far Cry. The expansive landscapes are not just pretty backdrops; they play a central role in the narrative. There are hidden stories, side quests, and unique encounters scattered throughout, inviting players to dive deeper into the story. By designing exploration mechanics that reward curiosity, game designers can create a more engaging storytelling experience. Encouraging players to uncover the narrative through exploration not only boosts their involvement but also gives them a sense of ownership over the story, allowing them to craft their own unique journey in the game.

Analyzing Narrative Techniques of Elden Ring

In Elden Ring, the way the story is told is cleverly designed to make players feel more connected to the game world. Rather than relying solely on traditional conversations or cutscenes, the game uses its environment to share its lore. Players can learn about the history of the Lands Between by exploring ruined castles, abandoned villages, and other interesting locations, inviting them to piece together the story themselves. This method not only fits well with the game's exploration style but also allows each player to interpret the story in their own personal way.

Another important storytelling technique in Elden Ring is its non-linear approach, where the story is told in bits and pieces. Players can find snippets of lore in item descriptions, conversations with non-playable characters (NPCs), and the world around them. This encourages exploration and a sense of discovery, as players can connect the dots in different ways. By creating stories that aren't straightforward, game designers can help players feel more involved and empowered to uncover the narrative at their own pace.

The interactions with NPCs in Elden Ring also enhance the storytelling. The game features well-developed characters whose backgrounds and motivations unfold based on players' choices and actions. This means that how players engage with these characters can shape the storyline, leading to different relationships and possible outcomes. By creating smart AI systems that respond to player behavior, designers can make the narrative experience more engaging and emotionally impactful.

Exploration is crucial to the story in Elden Ring. Players are encouraged to explore various landscapes, each filled with hidden secrets and challenges that enrich the overall plot. This approach not only rewards curiosity but also entwines gameplay with storytelling, making the act of exploring a significant part of the narrative. Game designers should think about how the design of the environment can help tell stories, guiding players on their journey while allowing them to discover and engage with the world in their own way.

Finally, Elden Ring showcases the power of having multiple pathways in its gameplay. Players can choose from various quests and objectives that can be tackled in different ways, leading to different endings based on their choices. This structure not only adds replay value but also allows players to customize their experience, creating a deeper connection to the story. By offering multiple paths, game designers can create an open world that values player choices and leads to rich storytelling experiences, resulting in a more immersive and emotionally rewarding game.

Analyzing Narrative Techniques of Zelda Breath of the Wild

Exploring the storytelling techniques in "Zelda: Breath of the Wild" offers valuable lessons for game designers creating open world games that balance freedom and a compelling story. In this game, the tale is intricately tied to a big, beautiful world, allowing players to discover the story naturally as they explore and interact with their surroundings. Unlike many games that follow a straight path in storytelling, Breath of the Wild lets players discover the history of Hyrule in a more open-ended way, using clues found in the environment, scattered memories, and conversations with different characters. This design choice encourages players to dive into the game, building emotional connections to the story based on their unique adventures.

One standout feature of Breath of the Wild is its environmental storytelling. The game's world is filled with traces of its past, like ancient ruins and hidden treasures, each adding to the overall story. This approach not only enriches the history of Hyrule but also invites players to explore at their own pace. Game designers can take inspiration from this by including details in their settings that help tell a story, making players feel more engaged with the world they're experiencing.

Interactions with non-playable characters (NPCs) in Breath of the Wild further showcase how to effectively weave narrative into an open world. Each character adds to the story in their own way, whether by offering quests, sharing insights, or providing lore that deepens the player's understanding of the world. The game features a smart system that allows for different interactions, meaning players can enjoy varied conversations and outcomes based on their choices. This highlights for designers the need to create rich NPCs that enhance the narrative, encouraging players to explore different aspects of the story.

The game takes players on a thrilling journey with its multi-path storyline, allowing them to make choices that significantly shape their adventure. Instead of following a single linear route, players can tackle challenges from various angles, leading to a multitude of unique experiences. This design not only invites exploration and experimentation but also captures the very essence of what open-world games are all about. Game developers should consider incorporating branching narratives that react to player decisions, creating a storytelling experience that feels deeply personal and immersive.

Moreover, Breath of the Wild truly shines when it comes to connecting with players on an emotional level. The themes of loss, hope, and healing resonate profoundly as players traverse the remnants of a fallen kingdom, all while striving to restore harmony. The personal stories of the Champions introduce emotional stakes that players gradually unveil throughout their quest. This highlights a crucial lesson for game designers: the power of weaving emotional depth into the narrative. By crafting relatable characters and presenting their struggles, designers can cultivate a richer connection between players and the game, resulting in greater engagement and satisfaction.

Analyzing Narrative Techniques of Ultima

In the world of "Ultima," the narrative techniques are not just tools; they are the very essence of an immersive experience that draws players into its captivating realm. One of the standout features is the intricately crafted world that responds to player choices, instilling a powerful sense of agency that's vital for any open-world adventure. Every environment in "Ultima" is far more than just a backdrop; it's a living, breathing element of the story. Each locale comes alive with its own lore and history, beckoning players to delve deeper and engage with the narrative on multiple layers. This interactive design fosters a profound connection between the player and the game world, ensuring that every journey feels uniquely personal.

Character development in "Ultima" takes center stage with a rich, multifaceted approach that amplifies emotional engagement. The NPCs you encounter aren't mere quest-givers; they are vibrant characters woven into the fabric of the overarching story, each with their own motivations and backstories waiting to be uncovered. This depth allows players to forge meaningful relationships and grapple with moral choices, paving the way for an emotional investment that enriches the gameplay experience. Game designers can learn from this by crafting intricate character arcs and dialogue systems that mirror player decisions, paving the way for rich, varied outcomes. This way, players will truly feel the weight of their choices, elevating the narrative impact to new heights.

Exploration mechanics in "Ultima" beautifully intertwine with storytelling, urging players to wander off the beaten path. The game rewards curiosity with hidden quests, untold lore, and unforgettable encounters that enhance the narrative tapestry. This design philosophy fosters a thrilling sense of discovery, making exploration a key component of player engagement. By weaving narrative elements into the exploration mechanics, designers can create a world that feels alive and responsive, where every venture holds the promise of a new story waiting to unfold. The artful balance between guided quests and open exploration empowers players to weave their own narratives while remaining tethered to the wider story.

The use of multi-path storylines in "Ultima" showcases a nonlinear gameplay style that honors player choice. Every decision made throughout the game leads to different outcomes, nurturing a profound sense of ownership over the narrative. This approach not only enhances replayability but also invites players to experience the story from diverse perspectives. Game designers should embrace branching storylines that open up various paths, ensuring every player's experience is distinct. By integrating systems that track player choices and adapt the storyline accordingly, designers can create a storytelling experience that feels truly individualized and impactful. Lastly, the narrative techniques in "Ultima" highlight the significance of embedding thematic elements that resonate with universal human experiences. Themes of morality, sacrifice, and the pursuit of freedom are interwoven throughout the narrative, creating a tapestry that players can deeply connect with emotionally. By embedding these themes in both gameplay and character interactions, designers can enrich the narrative experience, prompting players to reflect on their own values and choices. Aligning thematic depth with gameplay mechanics is key to crafting open-world games that prioritize exploration and freedom while delivering compelling stories that leave a lasting impression on players.

Analyzing Narrative Techniques of Watch Dogs

"Watch Dogs" masterfully weaves together a captivating narrative that enriches its open-world design, creating a vibrant tapestry of story and player agency. Set against the bustling backdrop of a meticulously crafted Chicago, the game doesn't just create a virtual playground—it invites players into a living, breathing commentary on surveillance, privacy, and the quest for personal freedom. As you navigate this urban landscape, you'll uncover a multitude of intertwining stories that emerge organically from your interactions, allowing the game to resonate with real-world issues.

At the heart of this immersive experience is Aiden Pearce, our complex protagonist. Aiden embodies the struggle of a vigilante wrestling with his pursuit of justice and the moral consequences that stem from his choices. The narrative unfolds through Aiden's personal goals and his relationships with various characters, each representing the game's thematic depth. This character-driven approach not only enhances emotional stakes but also opens the door to multi-faceted storylines. Your decisions shape Aiden's journey, encouraging you to reflect on the moral implications of each choice, which deepens your investment in the unfolding narrative.

The game also shines through its sophisticated AI systems, creating dynamic interactions with non-playable characters (NPCs) that elevate the story. These NPCs are more than mere background figures; they possess distinct personalities and respond meaningfully to Aiden's actions, highlighting the broader societal themes at play. This level of interaction allows you to engage with the world in a profound way—your choices influence how NPCs react, further shaping the narrative landscape uniquely for each player.

As you explore the vast open world, Watch Dogs rewards your curiosity with environmental storytelling and hidden narratives.

From collectibles to side missions, every corner of the city offers insights that deepen your understanding of the game's themes. Exploration transcends simple navigation; it becomes an essential part of the narrative journey, allowing you to piece together the larger story as you maneuver through the intricacies of the urban environment.

Finally, emotional engagement is a cornerstone of the game's narrative design. By presenting morally ambiguous situations and high-stakes dilemmas, "Watch Dogs" challenges you to confront your values and beliefs as you guide Aiden through his journey. The stakes feel real, and the consequences of your decisions weigh heavily on your conscience. Cinematic techniques—like beautifully crafted cutscenes and poignant dialogue—heighten the impact of crucial moments, creating a bond between you and the narrative.

Ultimately, "Watch Dogs" excels at demonstrating how powerful storytelling can elevate an open-world game, offering players a deeply personal and resonant experience that thoughtfully explores the complexities of freedom in today's digital age.

Lessons Learned from Industry Leaders

Insights from industry leaders in open world game design offer valuable guidance for new developers aiming to create engaging experiences that resonate with players. One key takeaway is the need for a strong story that works well with the gameplay. For example, in games like "The Witcher 3: Wild Hunt," players embark on a journey that is enriched by a richly detailed world filled with interesting stories and quests. Developers should focus on building a narrative that allows players to explore freely and make choices that feel meaningful.

Another important lesson is about using advanced technology to create interactive characters. Many successful games have shown that well-designed artificial intelligence (AI) can lead to characters that act in realistic ways based on how players engage with the game. In "Red Dead Redemption 2," for example, the game features non-playable characters (NPCs) that react differently depending on the player's actions and reputation, creating a more lifelike and interactive world. This suggests that developers should invest in AI that allows for more detailed interactions, adding depth to both storytelling and player involvement.

Exploration is also crucial in open world games, as it serves as a way to tell stories. Experts stress the importance of designing environments that spark curiosity and reward players for exploring. Games like "The Legend of Zelda: Breath of the Wild" highlight this by revealing stories through the scenery and hidden places. Developers should strive to create worlds that encourage players to investigate, filled with history and lore that gradually unfolds as they explore, thereby enhancing the overall narrative experience.

Emotional engagement is another important aspect. The ability to move players emotionally through their choices adds to the memorability of a game. Titles such as "Life is Strange" connect players to the story through moments that require tough decisions. Developers should aim to create multi-dimensional characters and situations that provoke genuine feelings, making sure that players care about the outcomes of their choices, not just the exploration itself.

Lastly, the idea of having multiple story paths in a game is a significant lesson. Many popular games feature branching narratives that allow players to shape their own experience, emphasizing the importance of player choice. For instance, "Cyberpunk 2077" showcases how decisions can lead to different endings, encouraging players to replay the game for a fresh experience. Developers should prioritize building intricate storylines that adapt to player choices, ensuring that every playthrough feels unique and reinforcing the freedom that makes open world games so appealing.

Innovations in Open World Design
In recent years, the way video games create open worlds has changed a lot, making it easier and more exciting for players to explore and enjoy the stories within the games. Game designers are now focused on building environments that not only invite

players to explore but also tell rich and engaging stories. This new way of designing open worlds highlights how important it is for players to have the freedom to make their own choices, allowing them to connect more deeply with the game's story and the world around them. By using creative new ideas and systems, designers can craft worlds that feel lively and responsive to what players do.

One major advancement is the use of smart technology for non-player characters (NPCs) in games. In older games, NPCs often acted in predictable ways, which could make them feel less interesting to the players. Now, thanks to new artificial intelligence (AI), these characters can behave in more surprising and realistic ways, responding to players' choices and actions. This makes the game feel more immersive, as players meet characters with distinct personalities that change based on their interactions. This improved storytelling helps players form emotional connections with the characters they meet, enriching their overall experience.

The way players explore open worlds has also improved, enhancing the storytelling aspect of games. Designers are trying out different ways to lead players through their environments that don't rely on strict paths. For instance, environmental storytelling uses the game's visuals and themes to communicate parts of the narrative, encouraging players to discover the story naturally. Interactive elements like artifacts or puzzles make exploration fun and meaningful, helping players uncover stories at their own pace and building a deeper bond with the game world.

Players' emotional experiences are heightened by meaningful choices that affect the game's story and environment. Designers are paying attention to how players' decisions can shape not only the storyline but also the game world itself. This leads to numerous possible outcomes and pathways, allowing players to see the real consequences of their actions as they play. When designers reflect these choices in significant ways, players feel a stronger sense of control and connection to the game, turning their gameplay into a personal journey where they care about the results of their decisions.

Lastly, the idea of multi-path storylines in games that

don't follow a straight line represents a significant innovation in open-world design. By letting players choose from different story threads, designers can create complex narratives that cater to different styles of play. This flexibility not only makes games more replayable but also encourages players to explore various aspects of the game world, leading to unique stories based on their choices. As game designers continue to innovate in open-world design, these advancements will lead to richer, more engaging experiences that value both storytelling and player freedom in exciting new ways.

Future Trends in Open World Game Design
Emerging Technologies and Their Impact

New technologies are changing the way open-world games are designed, offering exciting new ways to create engaging stories and interactions for players. Advances in artificial intelligence (AI), generating game content automatically, and virtual reality (VR) are giving game designers the tools to create experiences that feel more alive and immersive. With these technologies, designers can make characters that react more realistically and can create environments that change based on what players do.

AI is a key player in this shift, allowing characters in the game, known as non-player characters (NPCs), to show more realistic behavior and emotions. By using smart algorithms, designers can create NPCs that learn from what players do, making the game world feel more believable. When players feel like their choices truly matter and affect the game's outcome, they become more emotionally invested in the story. AI also helps create interactive dialogues, allowing for deeper connections between players and characters, enriching the game's narrative.

Additionally, the ability to automatically generate game content plays a big role in creating unique adventures. Designers can use algorithms to build vast and diverse landscapes, ensuring that players encounter something different each time they explore the game. This surprise element keeps players engaged and allows them to discover hidden stories and quests as they traverse these ever-changing environments.

Virtual reality brings a whole new level of immersion to open-world games. Players can physically move around and interact with the game world in ways that are simply not possible on regular platforms. This intense experience can lead to stronger emotional reactions, making players feel that their decisions have even more weight. Designers need to create easy-to-use controls and inviting settings that encourage exploration while keeping the story engaging.

The blend of these new technologies opens up exciting opportunities for creating stories that change based on player choices, allowing multiple endings and replay value. By combining AI, automated content creation, and VR, game designers can tell rich, complex stories that respond to how players act in real-time, crafting personal and expansive experiences. As these technologies continue to improve, the potential for storytelling in open-world games will expand, leading to richer and more satisfying experiences for players.

The Role of Community and Player Feedback

In the thrilling realm of open world game design, the impact of community and player feedback is nothing short of revolutionary! Designers must embrace the idea that players are not just passive consumers; they are dynamic co-creators of the game's story and mechanics. Players bring invaluable insights that can shine a light on gameplay elements that may have been overlooked during development, offering a fresh perspective on the world players inhabit. By actively engaging with their community, designers can collect vital information to refine gameplay, enhance storytelling, and elevate the overall experience to new heights.

Community feedback has the incredible power to shape the design of open world AI systems, especially in how non-playable characters (NPCs) interact with players. Players have their fingers on the pulse of immersion, providing feedback that reveals the intricacies of AI behavior. For example, they might crave more dynamic NPC reactions to player actions or shifts in the environment. This insight allows designers to push the envelope, implementing sophisticated AI systems that create a more vivid and believable world. When player input drives AI design, emotional engagement skyrockets, allowing players to forge deeper connections with characters and the unfolding narrative.

Exploration mechanics are the lifeblood of open world games, and player feedback is crucial in their successful development. Every player approaches exploration in their own unique way, and their experiences can uncover opportunities for truly innovative enhancements. Feedback may reveal areas where players feel boxed in or where mechanics fail to reward adventurous exploration. By continually refining these mechanics based on player insights, designers can craft a vibrant, living environment that invites discovery and interaction, ultimately amplifying the storytelling aspects of the game. This iterative evolution fosters an organic bond between players and the game world, paving the way for an immersive narrative journey.

Emotional player engagement hinges on the choices available in open world adventures. Community feedback provides a treasure trove of insight into how players perceive the weight of their decisions and the stakes involved in the unfolding story. Designers can tap into which choices resonate most profoundly with players, allowing them to enrich narrative paths and intensify emotional impact. By understanding the intricate emotional landscape players navigate, designers can develop complex multi-path storylines that mirror the rich tapestry of player experiences. This engagement not only deepens the narrative but also instills a sense of ownership in players, ensuring their choices truly shape the outcome.

Ultimately, the vibrant dialogue between game designers, players, and the community is essential for the ever-evolving landscape of open world games. By embracing and celebrating player feedback, designers can orchestrate thrilling, emotionally resonant experiences that champion freedom and narrative depth. This collaborative journey transforms games from static products into living entities that grow and thrive alongside their passionate player base. By valuing community input, designers can create worlds that are not only ripe for exploration and interaction but also ignite a profound passion for the stories waiting to be discovered!

Predictions for the Next Generation of Open Worlds

The future of open world video games is going to change in exciting ways as new technologies develop and we learn more about what players enjoy. One significant change will be the use of smart computer systems, known as artificial intelligence (AI), which will help create non-player characters (NPCs) that act and react in more realistic ways. This means that when players make choices in the game, those choices will feel like they truly matter and influence the world around them. The result will be a more engaging experience where players connect emotionally with the characters, making the game more immersive.

Exploration will also take on new importance in these future games. Players will not just wander through vast landscapes; they will unearth stories by interacting with the environment. Designers will build worlds where players can discover hidden tales and dialogues just by looking around and exploring. This approach will make exploring the game world feel directly tied to the story, giving players the freedom to advance the plot at their own pace.

Emotional connection will be vital to the next wave of open world games. As players want deeper, more meaningful interactions, game designers will focus on creating well-rounded characters with rich backgrounds and relatable motivations. Making choices that affect the story will add emotional weight to the gameplay—whether through conversations, personal challenges, or the outcomes of decisions. This emphasis on emotional depth will strengthen the bond between players and the game world.

Additionally, future games will feature storylines that branch off in multiple directions, allowing players to shape their unique experiences based on their choices. As technology makes it easier to create complex stories, designers will ensure that the decision-making process remains user-friendly. By allowing players to see the impact of their actions without feeling overwhelmed, games can encourage a sense of ownership over the story, leading to more replayable experiences.

In the end, the next generation of open world games will combine freedom with rich storytelling and emotional experiences. Game designers will need to harness new technologies to build vast worlds filled with interesting stories and deep interactions. By focusing on smart NPCs, innovative ways to explore, and emotionally engaging narratives, they can create gaming experiences that not only entertain but also inspire and connect players to the stories they play through. This exciting vision promises that players will enjoy a landscape where their choices seamlessly weave into the story, resulting in unforgettable gaming adventures.

Crafting Freedom in Game Design

Designing open-world games that focus on freedom and storytelling offers valuable insights into how players interact with narratives. Game creators need to understand that giving players freedom isn't just about having big, open worlds to explore. It's also about the important choices players face along the way. Each decision can influence the story, reflecting what players care about and how they feel. Therefore, it's important to combine a strong story with open-world gameplay. This way, players truly feel like they can shape their own adventures.

To make the game experience more engaging, using advanced technology to manage how characters (NPCs) interact with players is key. When NPCs react in a realistic way to player decisions, it makes the game world feel lively and responsive. These character interactions should change based on what players do, showing the impact of their choices. The challenge for developers is to ensure that these interactions don't just add variety but also deepen the story. NPCs should help tell the story by offering quests, sharing insights, or forming emotional connections with players, enhancing the overall gameplay and helping players feel more invested in the world.

Exploration is also crucial for storytelling in open-world

games. Designers need to think carefully about how players move around and what they learn during their adventures. Using techniques like environmental storytelling—where the setting itself shares narrative elements—can immerse players even more. Offering different ways to explore, such as climbing, swimming, or flying, lets players interact with the world naturally. Every discovery, whether it's a hidden quest or a piece of lore, adds to the story and gives meaning to the player's choices, making exploration an essential part of the narrative.

Emotional engagement is a significant aspect of the player experience. Open-world games can create opportunities for moments that evoke strong feelings. By presenting tough moral choices and important decisions, developers can encourage players to think about their own values and beliefs. These choices should not only affect the story in the moment but also have lasting effects throughout the game, impacting relationships with NPCs and altering the overall storyline. This emotional connection helps players feel a sense of responsibility and attachment to the game's outcome.

Using multi-path storylines in non-linear gameplay further strengthens the idea of freedom in game design. Allowing players to choose different story routes creates rich and varied narratives that cater to different play styles. Each path should provide unique experiences and consequences, encouraging players to explore different angles of the story. This approach not only enhances replayability but also empowers players to connect with the game world meaningfully. In the end, crafting freedom in game design is about more than just having open spaces; it's about creating a blend of choices, consequences, and stories that resonate with players on many levels.

Recap of key points regarding open world design

Open world design is all about giving players the freedom to explore and make choices, which creates a rich storytelling experience. It's important for game designers to find a good balance between letting players roam freely and guiding them with a clear story. This balance helps players feel free to follow what interests them while still keeping track of the overall plot. When done well, open worlds invite players to engage in a way that feels rewarding and helps them connect deeply with the game.

A big part of what makes an open world engaging is the use of smart AI systems that let players interact meaningfully with characters that aren't controlled by other players (called NPCs). These interactions should be lively and responsive, so NPCs can react based on what players do. When NPC behavior is more realistic, it makes the game world feel alive and draws players in even more. By creating AI that adapts to players' choices, designers can build a vibrant world that encourages exploration and experimentation, adding depth to the story.

Exploration plays a crucial role in storytelling in open-world games. Designers need to think about how players will uncover different parts of the story through the environments, quests, and hidden details. By incorporating diverse ways to explore, like climbing, swimming, or driving vehicles, players can experience a wider variety of gameplay, which also helps them connect with the story. These exploration features should blend smoothly into the game world, allowing players to find secrets and create their own paths, resulting in a unique narrative experience that resonates emotionally.

The decisions players make in an open world can greatly influence their emotional connection to the game. These choices should lead to clear consequences that affect the game's world and story. Designers can achieve this by offering branching storylines and dynamic environments that change based on player actions. When players have multiple story paths to choose from, they feel a greater sense of ownership over their journey, which deepens their emotional engagement. The relationship between choice and consequence is key to creating a story that feels dynamic and responsive.

Lastly, allowing for multiple story paths is essential in open world gameplay. Players should be able to experience different aspects of the story depending on their choices, resulting in varied endings and experiences. This approach not only increases the replay value of the game but also strengthens players' connection to the narrative. Designers should aim to create a world where every decision, no matter how small, can influence the story, so players feel like their actions truly matter. By focusing on these elements, game designers can craft open world experiences that are both immersive and rich in storytelling.

Emphasizing the balance between player autonomy and story

In the world of open-world video games, it's important to find the right balance between giving players the freedom to explore and keeping the story interesting. Today's players want the chance to wander through game worlds, make choices, and interact with characters in their own way. However, this freedom shouldn't come at the cost of a good storyline. Game designers need to create experiences where players can choose their own paths while still being drawn into a captivating narrative. This balance is crucial for keeping players engaged and satisfied with their gaming experience.

At its heart, player freedom means allowing gamers to make choices that impact their journey and the virtual world around them. This can happen in various ways, like customizing characters, choosing dialogue options, or deciding how a quest unfolds. But if players are given too much freedom without a strong story framework, the game can feel chaotic and lose its emotional depth. Designers should create guiding structures within the story that help players navigate their adventure while still allowing them to express themselves. This can be done by embedding key story elements throughout the game world for players to discover at their own pace.

To improve storytelling in open-world games, using smart systems for interacting with characters is essential. Intelligent non-playable characters (NPCs) can respond to player choices in meaningful ways, adding realism and depth to the game. For example, an NPC might react differently to a player based on their previous interactions. This dynamic storytelling makes players feel like their choices truly influence the game world, enhancing their sense of involvement and agency.

Exploration is also very important in telling stories

within open-world settings. Designers should encourage players to explore not just to find hidden treasures but also to engage with the game's narrative. By incorporating environmental storytelling, hidden lore, and collectible items, players can gain a deeper understanding of the game world and its characters. This multi-layered approach can increase players' emotional investment as they uncover the stories linked to their surroundings.

Lastly, allowing for multiple paths in a non-linear story structure enables players to experience different parts of the narrative based on their choices. This approach honors the players' freedom and highlights the significance of their decisions in shaping the story. By offering various outcomes and consequences, designers can create a more immersive experience that resonates emotionally with players. The real challenge is to ensure that each storyline remains engaging, featuring rich character journeys and satisfying endings that encourage exploration and involvement. Striking this balance will lead to a more rewarding and memorable gaming experience, where players feel both free and integral to the unfolding story.

Final thoughts on the importance of compelling world-building in narrative experiences

Creating an engaging world is a fundamental aspect of making open-world video games enjoyable and memorable. A well-designed game world serves as a rich backdrop for players' adventures, encouraging them to explore, engage with its elements, and become deeply involved in the unfolding story. When a game world feels alive and responsive—complete with dynamic weather systems, day-night cycles, and evolving ecosystems—it can significantly enhance players' experiences and emotional investment. For game designers, mastering the art of building these immersive environments is crucial for crafting narratives that resonate powerfully with players.

At its core, world-building involves meticulously assembling the details of the game universe, which includes its intricate history, diverse geography, unique cultures, and the vibrant characters that inhabit it. Designers must strike a delicate balance—providing enough depth and detail to intrigue players without overwhelming them with excessive information. Effective world-building not only stimulates player curiosity but also fosters a sense of belonging, making their choices feel impactful and significant. It's essential for designers to consider how every facet of the game world contributes to the overarching story, allowing players to gradually uncover new layers of narrative through exploration and interaction.

The role of characters, particularly non-playable characters (NPCs), within these worlds is immensely important. These characters should serve more than just a decorative purpose; they should augment the storytelling experience by offering quests, revealing lore, and establishing meaningful emotional connections with players. Leveraging advanced technology, such as artificial intelligence and procedural generation, can enable these characters to interact in nuanced ways that adapt to player actions, fostering a sense of agency and immersion. This higher level of interactivity allows players to cultivate stronger bonds with the game, encouraging them to explore and connect with the story on a more personal level.

Exploration itself is another vital dimension of storytelling in open-world games. By meticulously designing environments that reward curiosity—such as hidden treasures, lore-rich locations, and intriguing side quests—designers can empower players to feel that their decisions carry real weight and consequences. This sense of freedom invites players to forge their own narrative paths, ensuring that each player's journey feels unique and significant, ultimately enriching their overall gaming experience.

Creating immersive worlds is the heartbeat of narrative-driven games, and it's what makes player experiences truly unforgettable. When game designers invest in strong world-building, they aren't just setting the stage—they're crafting a vibrant universe filled with emotional connections and rich stories just waiting to be discovered. By designing intricate environments alongside dynamic characters, they invite players to embark on thrilling journeys of exploration and adventure. This thoughtful combination not only captivates players but also resonates deeply, turning each gaming session into a memorable experience that lingers long after the screen goes dark. Dive in, explore, and let the story unfold!